WHO ARE YOU...
Uninterrupted?

UNLOCKING YOUR SUBCONSCIOUS
POWER

WRITTEN BY
STEPHANIE 'LIBERTY' FRANCOIS

The Finest
Invites readers to break free from the chains of limiting beliefs, to nurture an optimistic heart, and to discover peace amidst life's whirlwind. It's a journey of answering your soul's deepest call, mastering the art of living with intention and grace.

Acknowledgement

I would like to express my deepest gratitude to all those who have supported and inspired me throughout the creation of this book. To my family, whose unwavering encouragement has been a constant source of strength, and to my friends, who have always believed in the importance of this journey, I am indebted to your unwavering support.
A special thanks to the countless individuals who have shared their personal stories of self-discovery and empowerment with me. Your experiences have enriched the content of this book and serve as a reminder that we are all on this path of understanding who we are…uninterrupted.

I would also like to extend my appreciation to the dedicated professionals and experts whose insights and knowledge have contributed to the depth of this work. Your guidance has been invaluable. And finally, to the readers, it is your curiosity, your thirst for self-improvement, and your belief in the potential of the human spirit that drive the existence of this book. May your journey within these pages be transformative, enlightening, and empowering.
With heartfelt thanks,

PROLOGUE

In the busy noise of everyday life, we can easily forget who we really are. The world around us bombards us with distractions, expectations, and external pressures that often drown out the voice of our inner selves. But deep within, beyond the noise and the chaos, there lies a reservoir of untapped potential—the subconscious mind—a powerful force that holds the key to understanding who you are, uninterrupted.

Welcome to "Who Are You Uninterrupted?: Unlocking Your Subconscious Power." This book is an exploration of the profound journey of self-discovery and empowerment that awaits you. It's a guide to navigating the depths of your own mind, unearthing the hidden treasures within, and unleashing your true potential. The steps outlined in these pages are not just a collection of theories; they are a roadmap to understanding the enigmatic subconscious mind and utilizing its power to transform your life. This book will take you on a voyage of self-exploration, helping you to recognize the subconscious patterns that have shaped your existence and guiding you in reprogramming them to align with your deepest desires and aspirations.
But why should you embark on this journey, and why should you choose this book?

Why This Book Matters:

- **Rediscover Yourself:** In the hustle and bustle of life, we often lose sight of our true selves. This book offers a chance to reconnect with your innermost thoughts, feelings, and aspirations, allowing you to rediscover who you are at your core.

- **Empowerment:** Understanding and harnessing the power of your subconscious mind can be a game-changer. It empowers you to take control of your life, make conscious choices, and overcome obstacles that may have held you back.

- **Real-Life Transformation:** The steps in this book are not mere theories but practical tools that have transformed the lives of countless individuals. Through their stories and experiences, you'll witness the tangible impact of these practices.

- **A Holistic Approach:** This book combines scientific insights with practical exercises, providing a comprehensive approach to subconscious reprogramming. It caters to both those seeking a better understanding of the mind's inner workings and those eager to take actionable steps towards self-improvement.

- **A Community of Explorers:** By delving into the pages of this book, you join a community of like-minded individuals on a similar quest for self-discovery. Your journey is not solitary; it is a shared experience with countless others seeking to unlock their potential.

This book is an invitation to embark on a transformative journey—a journey that promises to reveal who you are uninterrupted and empowers you to rewrite the story of your life. It's a journey filled with self-discovery, empowerment, and the realization of your untapped potential. Are you ready to unlock the doors to your subconscious and step into a world of limitless possibilities? If so, let's begin.

CHAPTER ONE

THE QUEST WITHIN

SELF DISCOVERY

CHAPTER 1

THE QUEST WITHIN

"Guiding you toward the reservoir of untapped potential within"

Have you ever wondered who you really are?
What your life purpose is? What are you really meant to do on this Earth, in this lifetime? Do you feel that there is more to you and what you can offer? If you are still searching for these answers, then you have come to the right place. The journey of self-discovery requires a lot of groundwork and can be daunting at times, as it involves revisiting a lot of your past experiences, choices and emotions. Therefore, this book will guide you through all the details you require in your journey to unravel your true self. This includes identifying your personality, awakening your spiritual dimension, learning to love yourself as well as embracing the change that comes. It will no doubt trigger confusion, doubt, and misunderstandings, which will force you to make decisions that will affect your life. However you need to trust the process as it is worth taking and you will turn out to be an entirely different person from where you started off.

There is more to you than you think. Let go of your past and focus on what is about to come. Give yourself permission go through this journey and allow yourself to be vulnerable. When you open up yourself to all the possibilities this journey will bring, you will realize how rewarding it is at the end. You will discover the most important element of all: **YOURSELF**. The journey of self-discovering who you are… *uninterrupted* starts with a single step - the courage to take an honest look within. We often go through life on autopilot, soaked in roles and routines that leave little room for self-reflection. But somewhere deep inside, a small voice is calling from a distance, urging you to peel away the layers and uncover who you truly are. It's time to finally listen. This journey will lead you to spaces within that may seem unfamiliar, even uncomfortable. You'll find beliefs and patterns so deep-rooted you never thought to question them. But now you must. As you explore the landscape of your inner world, have compassion. The ways you've coped and survived up to now were necessary. But the time has come to shed what no longer serves you, and step into your power. The first step in this self-reflection is honest self-assessment. So, You ready to set off on an epic quest to uncover the real you, without any interruptions? Cool, grab your journal and let's make something shake. Describe yourself, your personality, your quirks. Don't hold back – get specific. What are your best and worst traits? How do others perceive you? Now go deeper. What energizes you? What bores you? What are your secret passions and what fills you with dread? As patterns emerge, contemplate the origins. Our childhoods and upbringing shape us profoundly. The beliefs we subconsciously absorbed back then continue directing our lives today. This self-assessment shines a light so you can finally update outdated programming. Keep jotting down in your journal to find more hidden treasures about yourself. Write about what you feel, what you do, how you react. Surprising insights will pop up, like unexpected plot twists in your favorite show. The real you is waiting just beneath the surface, ready for its grand debut. This isn't just about learning your personality or habits; it's a journey to the soul. Underneath the hustle of everyday life, there's a quieter, more profound part of you, just itching to be discovered.

And that's precisely what 'Who Are You, Uninterrupted' is all about. It's an invitation to pause the noise of life, to step away from the distractions, and truly meet yourself. In these pages, you're not just discovering facts about yourself; you're uncovering the unfiltered, unpaused essence of who you are. It's a journey to find the you that exists when the world isn't watching, when the roles and expectations are stripped away. So, as you turn each page and write each word, remember, you're not just filling out a journal. You're exploring the vast, uncharted territory of your true self, uninterrupted.

Make time and space for your inner world. Meditate, walk in nature, listen to music – do anything that soothes your spirit and helps you tune out external noise. In these moments, you may find truths about yourself that feel like coming home. There are many paths to explore this inner landscape. For some, spiritual practices provide a conduit. For others, therapy and coaching help navigate inner spaces. How you choose to access this deeper dimension is personal. Discover what truly appeals to you and dedicate yourself to it. Your heart's deepest desires deserves your attention. As your true self comes into focus, pieces of the puzzle connect. You've got the hang of looking after your spirit now. You're back in the driver's seat, knowing exactly what you need to flourish. This newfound understanding of yourself starts to make waves in all parts of your life. You find your true calling again. Those passions you tucked away long ago? They start to shine through, showing you they're the secret ingredients to your happiness. You become a pro at tuning out anything that doesn't jive with your deepest truths. And guess what? Joy and purpose begin to fill your days, making every moment count. The process of shedding and unlearning is ongoing, but liberation emerges as you progressively honor your authentic self. You discover that seeking approval from others doesn't hold a candle to the power of loving yourself. Comparison loses its grip as you appreciate your uniqueness. No longer swayed by should's and expectations, you trust your inner compass to guide you. Finding who your are uninterrupted grants you authority over your life. This journey isn't always smooth. At times, discomfort arises as old stories unravel. Fears surface, asking you to soothe yourself with compassion, not judgement. Breakthroughs follow breakdowns. Each step ahead requires the courage and faith to push beyond growing edges into uncharted territory. Yet with your discoveries, you gain the tools to navigate uncertainty with perseverance. The wisdom you've earned from your own experiences outshines any outside counsel. You get to know your own complexities and gifts on a deeper level. Above all, remember you won't walk this road alone. Others like myself have ventured here before you. Lessons left behind light the way. Guidance and support exist at every turn for those bold enough to embark on the quest to meet their inner selves. Your journey of discovering who you are uninterrupted has already begun. With each step, you'll access more of your power and potential. Possibilities you've only dreamt of will unfold. Are you ready to uncover the real you? If so, let's make it happen. A world of insight and transformation awaits within.

CHAPTER TWO

THE UNVEILING

WHO ARE YOU?

CHAPTER 2

THE UNVEILING

"A journey best walked without the echoes of others' footsteps"

Your subconscious mind is a powerful place for change. Under our everyday thoughts, there's a deep inner world we haven't completely discovered yet. In this deep realm, outside the spotlight of our attention, incredible forces shape our realities. Imagine your mind as an iceberg. The conscious mind is simply the tip peeking above the water. Meanwhile, invisible below the surface, the subconscious accounts for the massive, hidden parts. This underwater portion of our minds is many times more extensive, powerful, and influential than the conscious tip. But since it works in the background, its influence on our lives is mostly hidden. It's time to reveal this hidden force behind your experiences and choices. As you dive below the depths of consciousness, you'll discover just how profoundly your subconscious directs your existence. First and foremost, your subconscious mind is where your deepest beliefs, instincts, and emotional patterns reside. Over your life, you gather many expeviences, starting when you're young. This creates a pattern in your subconscious that works on its own, shaping how you see things, think, and react. It's like a built-in GPS, guiding your life based on these deep-seated patterns. With such an enormous influence over your choices and behaviors, gaining awareness of these subconscious drivers is essential. Start observing your gut feelings and emotional responses. Do certain situations trigger you time and again? Do fearful beliefs limit your potential? Your reactions reveal the contents of your subconscious mind. By growing your self-awareness, you shed light on the hidden forces within you. Yet shining a light is just the initial step. When you notice your subconscious habits, you can change them on purpose. Through tools like meditation, visualization and affirmations, you can effectively reprogram your inner world. Meditation quiets your busy conscious mind, opening a gateway directly to the subconscious realm. Here, you can implant new visions of what you wish to manifest. Creative visualization is powerful for setting goals. Picture in detail, what you desire to achieve or become. Repeatedly impress these vivid scenes upon the subconscious mind. Meanwhile, affirmative mantras help instill new beliefs to supplant limiting old ones. Repeating empowering phrases daily will, over time, dissolve negative programming that restricted you. With consistent practice, you can gain authority over this autonomous inner domain that silently commands your outcomes. The vast untapped potential within these depths awaits your direction.

Yet be aware that subconscious reprogramming requires patience and commitment. These habitual mental patterns took years to solidify; modifying them takes time and effort. But persistence pays exponential dividends. As you consciously harness the power of your subconscious mind, your goals and dreams will progressively manifest from latent potential into tangible form. Breakthroughs become more frequent. Your power to create your reality amplifies dramatically. Those who succeed at high levels all intuitively learn to master their subconscious minds. By following their lead, your life already begins magically transforming.

Keep observing your thoughts, beliefs and reactions. This alertness helps you spot unhelpful thought patterns as they happen, enabling you to actively transform your inner landscape. Celebrate how far you've come while continuing to deepen your practice. With each repetition of your visualizations, affirmations, and meditations, you strengthen the new neural pathways that will soon dominate your inner landscape. What once seemed fixed and rigid, yields to the persistent power of focused awareness and intention. No matter your previous challenges, remember the subconscious mind created them, which means it can also resolve them. Step by step, as you overcome these limiting beliefs, you free yourself to claim the life you truly deserve. This process requires dedication, courage and self-trust. Yet the joy, fulfillment and sense of empowerment you'll feel is profoundly worth the effort. Be patient but persistent. Your subconscious patterns likely took decades to take root. They cannot transform overnight. But they absolutely can transform. Keep observing unhelpful emotional reactions and ask, "Why does this trigger me?" Trace it back to an underlying subconscious belief. Then deliberately replace fear with faith. Exchange lack for abundance. Transform trauma into growth. You hold the tools to cultivate an empowering inner garden where once only weeds grew. With care and patience, the soil of your subconscious mind will blossom into a landscape of possibility. This process of tending to your inner world may feel foreign at first. We rarely peer behind the veil of consciousness separating seen from unseen. But the more you develop this awareness, the more natural it becomes. You establish an evolving dialogue with your subconscious mind. As you learn its language, entirely new channels of communication open within you. You understand how your subconscious expresses itself symbolically in dreams and intuition. You easily make sense of each subtle metaphor, uncovering guidance that was once concealed. In stillness, the answers you seek unveil themselves. As your vision clears, you learn to work in perfect harmony with your inner strength, instead of against it. Your conscious and subconscious minds unite, becoming conduits for your highest potential. You realize the mind that created your limitations and suffering also contains the seeds of your liberation. Everything you require to fulfill your soul's purpose lives within you. These undiscovered gifts await only your willingness to brave the depths. The landscape of your subconscious mind promises a journey beyond your wildest dreams. But prepare, for there be demons lurking. Unconscious programs that once served you may fight to maintain their control. When challenges arise, remember life provides them to strengthen - not stop - you. Trust in your quiet inner power, greater than any adversary. Keep pushing forward. Every step you take brings you nearer to the life you've dreamed of, a life that's yours for the taking. You're prepared now. A fresh start is on the horizon in the realm of your inner self. Move ahead with bravery and attention. Beneath lies your fate, inviting you to discover who you are *uninterrupted.*

Becoming Who You Desire To Be

Developing your personality is an incredible journey that can elevate you to heights beyond your wildest dreams. It touches and transforms different aspects of your life, including your social interactions, financial stability, and emotional wellness. But to embark on this path of personality development, the first step is to understand and recognize your unique personality.

- What type of personality are you?
- What are the strong and weak points in your personality traits?
- What are you doing to improve on your weaker traits and what initiatives are you
taking to enhance your strong points?

Answering these questions truthfully is the first step towards authentic self-realization. Begin by spending quality time alone. This is vital for connecting with your uninterrupted self, exploring the depths of your true personality. Then, chart your path towards self-improvement. Recognize both your strengths and weaknesses, and set goals that are realistic yet challenging. Strive for balance; being overly critical or too lenient can impede your journey.

Embrace forgiveness. Forgive yourself for all the mistakes you have ever committed in life. Trying to find yourself with a grudge and a bitter attitude towards yourself will be useless and will garner no results, as your mind and attitude are hindered by the past. Viewing past failures as lessons paves the way for future triumphs. Embody flexibility in your quest for self-growth. A rigid approach is counterproductive; be open to evolving your goals as you progress. Harmonize your entire being with this journey of personal evolution for smoother progress.

Visualizing your aspirations can clarify your path. Creating mental images or tangible representations of your objectives helps maintain focus and direction. Establish a routine with daily checklists and set your aims in achievable stages. This methodical approach ensures consistent, realistic progress towards discovering who you are *uninterrupted*.

"You must be the change you wish to see in the world"
- Mahatma Gandhi

How to Reach Your Goals

Each person we meet is distinct, shaped by their own unique blend of characteristics and behaviors. Our individual personalities set us apart, making each of us one-of-a-kind. These personalities are crafted from various factors. Firstly, we inherit certain traits from our parents and relatives. That's why you might notice similarities in your preferences and behaviors with those of your family members. Alongside inherited traits, we also develop characteristics throughout our lives. Our upbringing plays a crucial role here. The habits, values, and beliefs we adopt as children often leave a more lasting impact than those acquired in adulthood.

To effectively enhance your personality in a way that supports your goals, start by understanding your own personality type. Acknowledge your strengths and weaknesses honestly. If you're naturally outgoing and confident, leverage these traits to propel your career and aspirations. On the other hand, it's crucial to confront your weaknesses head-on. For instance, if you often find yourself battling negative thoughts, actively seek ways to cultivate a more positive outlook.

Remember, personal growth is about building on what you're already good at while also addressing areas that need improvement. By doing so, you pave the way towards achieving your goals and unlocking your full potential.

"The only way to deal with this life meaningfully is to find your passion and give yourself to it."
- Travis Smiley

Knowing Your Personality

There are many ways in identifying your personality type. Nowadays there are various online personality tests made available for you where the results can be accumulated within minutes. Personality types are classified into different categories, but generally there are four different temperaments – the introverted and the extroverted, the one who thinks and the one who feels, the one who uses judgment to conclude and the one who uses keenness, and finally, the one who prefers using senses and the one who uses discernment. These different temperaments usually determine how one will react to various situations and the choices one will make. When you have identified your personality type, you get better understanding of yourself.

You are able to maximize your potential and use it to your advantage. For instance, if you are introvert you can channel your talents in ways that suits your personality best. Knowing your personality type helps clear up how you communicate with others. You'll learn to adapt and complement the person you're interacting with. For example, you might be someone who carefully thinks things through and pays attention to details, while your friend might rely on spontaneity and quick decisions. This creates harmonious relationships.

"Character is power." - Booker T. Washington

Tips On Personality Development

Everyone has traits that make them unique and that make one David totally different from the other David, though they share the same name. These traits are what sets individuals apart. Our upbringing and the people we interact with play a significant role in shaping our personalities. Being truthful with yourself is must. It allows you to recognize both your strengths and weaknesses, enabling you to use them to your benefit. Enhancing your listening skills is also vital, a subtle art that can make a world of difference. By focusing more on listening than speaking, you'll gain insights that are invaluable for personal growth. When you do speak, steer clear of a self-centered approach. Being overly focused on oneself can hinder your development in becoming a well-rounded individual.

CHAPTER THREE

INNER CHORUS

VOICES IN YOUR HEAD

CHAPTER 3

INNER CHORUS

"Echo the truths of your undisturbed soul."

Unconditional self-love is the cornerstone of discovering who you truly are. But for many, loving oneself doesn't come easily. Instead, there's a constant search for approval from others, a relentless quest to prove worthiness, always feeling inadequate. Remember, you're not alone in this struggle. Society often teaches us that our worth is tied to our appearance, actions, or achievements. However, relying on external validation for self-worth only leads to a sense of emptiness. True self-discovery starts when you recognize your inherent value – just for being yourself. Once you do this, the need for external benchmarks falls away. You become free from the shackles of perceived imperfections, embracing all aspects of yourself with kindness and empathy.

This path towards self-love involves confronting and disarming those critical internal voices. Acknowledge their attempts to protect you, but firmly let them know they are no longer needed. Replace them with a nurturing, compassionate inner dialogue. Talk to yourself with the same

17

tenderness and understanding you would offer to a cherished child. Treat yourself as you wish others would treat you. Each morning, give thanks for your body housing your spirit for another precious day on Earth, Embrace the idea that everyday is another gift. Express gratitude for qualities you admire in yourself. What do you appreciate about your personality or values? What are your talents and strengths? When you notice self-criticism arising, pause and ask, "Would I speak this way to someone I love?" Then reassure yourself as you would that person. Imagine your heart as a wellspring of unconditional love that flows uninterruptedly. Just as a flower blossoms from a seed encoded with its beauty, you were born inherently worthy. Circumstances and people may have obscured this truth, but your light remains undimmed within. Let self-love gently uncover and revive it. Making this sacred practice a daily ritual lays the foundation upon which your highest self can flourish. Self-love crowns you with dignity, creating space to hear your soul's calling. As you honor your true nature, your dreams can safely take wing. When you commit fully to self-love, your life transforms. You welcome each new morning as a fresh canvas, excited for possibilities. Difficult emotions become teachers rather than tyrants. You move through the world unencumbered by others' expectations, centered in your wholeness. This unflinching self-acceptance fortifies you to weather life's storms. You forgive yourself for not meeting unrealistic standards, perfectionism replaced by understanding. Failures become feedback for future growth.

With less energy spent judging yourself, you have capacity to realize your talents. You embrace your quirks with amusement rather than shame. More moments feel vibrant and fulfilling. You become a safe harbor for yourself, dissolving the search for validation through work, relationships, achievement or appearance. At last you know your worth, unchanging and innate. You devote your one life to passion, not proving. When self-love flourishes, you magnetize love from others by reflecting back their own light. Your joy and contentment are contagious. You shine as one who has chosen to experience life's fullness. This journey requires courage to confront painful programming that distorts how you see yourself. But true power comes from shedding facades to stand tall in your truth. With kindness and patience, you midwife your highest self into being. On this path, you may stumble. Self-doubt tries to sabotage most when you draw closest to breakthroughs. Recommit each time you forget your worth, for you are still undoing a lifetime of untruths. Be gentle with your learning. You may feel selfish or conceited for focusing inward. Remember your loving service to the world flows from self-love, not self-sacrifice. Fill yourself first before pouring into others. When you embrace your wholeness, perfection becomes nonsensical. You understand hearts only break open to hold more light. Love saturates all you are. Your life becomes a gift you can finally cherish. The greatest love affair of your life is with yourself. All other loves illuminate this central relationship which gives them deeper meaning. In loving you completely, you have everything you need. You are ready to encounter your full potential. Your purpose and passions unveil themselves when you relate to yourself with reverence and care. Making this sacred covenant liberates you into a life vibrant with possibility. Today, begin putting first the yourself you have neglected for too long. You are ready to answer your spirit's call. You were born worthy; now, live accordingly. At your core, you are love.

This truth, once discovered, sets you free to flourish. Embrace it - and yourself - with your whole heart.

"It's the repetition of affirmations that leads to belief. And once that belief becomes a deep conviction, things begin to happen" -Muhammad Ali

The Presence Of A Subconscious Mind

Many believe they have complete control over their lives, yet overlook the significant influence of the subconscious mind. The truth is, not everything is within our control, including the workings of our subconscious. This part of our mind can be a double-edged sword. Unknowingly, many allow their subconscious to focus on negative thoughts, sometimes leading to severe consequences like depression or even suicide. This is just one way it manifests.

We naturally tend to lean towards negativity more than positivity. Do you remember the day you lose someone? In most cases, the answer will be yes. What comes after this is the affirmation of your feeling, be it positive or negative. Your response to events, positive or negative, is deeply influenced by your subconscious acceptance of these experiences. Expecting positive outcomes can often lead to them, just as expecting negative results can bring them to fruition. This happens because your subconscious mind has embraced these expectations as reality. The role of the subconscious is crucial in shaping our perceptions and self-presentation. When channeled positively, it can transform your life significantly. Given its deep connection to our emotions and feelings, nurturing a positive mindset in the subconscious is key to overcoming negativity and aiding in the journey of self-healing and growth, again, helping us discover who we are, *uninterrupted*.

"Follow your instincts. That's where true wisdom manifests itself" -Oprah Winfrey

A Key to Self-Discovery
In our daily lives, we often engage in internal dialogues, wrestling with the different 'voices' that surface in these moments. This phenomenon, known as self-talk, reflects our subconscious mind communicating with and often answering itself. These inner voices and the conclusions they lead us to play a crucial role in shaping our decisions. But the question remains: how reliable is our subconscious and the self-talk it generates?

Typically, self-talk kicks in around specific activities or events. It could be triggered by something we see, hear, or experience. While we consciously consider a situation, our subconscious is also at work. For example, thinking about an upcoming exam might prompt our subconscious to remind us to study - a form of positive self-talk that can be transformative.

Yet, there are times when self-talk can lead to negative outcomes. In the same scenario, rather than motivating us to prepare, it might induce anxiety, resulting in rushed decisions. Our perceptions, shaped by our current emotional state, can influence the nature of our self-talk. Identifying whether these internal conversations are based on facts or skewed perceptions is crucial for making better choices. Understanding and guiding our subconscious dialogues can be a vital step in the journey of self-discovery.

Achieve Success Using Subconscious Mind

The simple answer is yes, you can achieve success through your subconscious mind. The real question is 'How do you harness the subconscious mind to achieve success?' Our minds possess the remarkable ability to generate and project imagination. The creation of any imaginative concept begins in the conscious mind. Here, you control your desires and intentions, which are then transferred to the subconscious mind. The subconscious mind takes over to imagine, visualize, perceive, and feel. This transformative process is what drives motivation and propels individuals towards their desired successes. Effectively using your subconscious mind opens the door to numerous benefits. Maintaining a positive mindset throughout this process is vital. It ensures that your subconscious works in alignment with your positive intentions. It is estimated that humans typically utilize only about 15% of their subconscious potential. Imagine the possibilities if we could tap into the remaining 85%. The world could see less suffering and more peace, with individuals achieving success in various aspects of life.

To maximize the use of your subconscious mind, it's essential to understand yourself, learn the correct methods, and take command of this powerful mental resource. Remember, it's the shift from negative to positive subconscious thinking that lays the foundation for success. Embracing positivity is the key to unlocking the full potential of your subconscious mind.

Control of Your Subconscious Mind

The subconscious mind, a complex and often elusive part of our psyche, is challenging to comprehend. Those who manage to understand it do so by engaging with their inner voices. It's the part of our brain where our emotions and feelings reside, intertwined with our deepest insecurities. Though complete mastery may be challenging, uninterrupted focus and effort, can still gracefully influence your subconscious mind to some extent using thoughtful and specific techniques. One effective approach is using physical reminders. For example, if your goal is weight loss, create a list of do's and don'ts. This list could be written in a journal, on a piece of paper, or even displayed on your wall. These constant visual cues serve as repetitive reminders, helping steer your subconscious mind towards your goal.

Meditation is the second step to control your subconscious mind. It may be hard to concentrate during the initial days, but with time, you can achieve it. In meditation, you do not visualize anything; you just concentrate on your thoughts, by emptying it. All you have to do is first, relax yourself. Close your eyes and gather all your thoughts to a single point of concentration. Then release it, while maintaining the relaxed composure. This helps to rationalize your decision-making process.

Visualization is the third step. Once you managed to concentrate on meditation, now is the time to visualize your goals. This step gives you the motivation to achieve your goal. The more you visualize it, the more you are prone to work harder to achieve it. After all these steps, make promises to someone you trust so that you are holding yourself accountable on your goal. Inevitably, you will often receive both positive and negative feedbacks from them. If you tackle it using an optimistic attitude, the negative feedback will serve as an urge to deliver the promises.

"Your thoughts are the seeds you plant in the garden of your mind. Water them with belief, and watch your dreams bloom into reality." - Denzel Washington

Change Your Life

Now that you understand how your subconscious mind operates, it becomes simpler to develop positive habits. Take, for instance, an addiction to drinking – it's a habit formed and reinforced by your subconscious. Comprehending the mechanics behind it to change your life for the better. Research indicates a strong link between our subconscious and our habits. The key factor to consider is the gradual development of these habits. They didn't form overnight but evolved through repeated actions or thoughts, eventually becoming second nature. Each time you repeat an action or thought, it imprints on your subconscious and eventually becomes a regular part of your routine – a habit.

To change or control a habit, employ the same principle of repetition, but with a focus on positivity. Even in negative surroundings, maintaining a positive outlook is essential.

Being able to discern what's beneficial and what's harmful empowers you to manage your habits effectively.

"Your subconscious mind is a treasure trove of wisdom. Listen to its whispers, and you'll find the answers you seek." - Maya Angelou

Mastering Solutions

Once you recognize how your habits are intertwined with your subconscious, it's time to harness this connection to find solutions. Believing in your subconscious mind's power is crucial for tapping into its full potential. So, how do you effectively engage your subconscious mind? Here are some methods to help you utilize it for problem-solving.

First, clearly communicate your challenges to your subconscious. Approach this with a positive mindset, focusing on finding solutions. Regularly remind your subconscious of these issues, emphasizing the quest for answers. Visualizing the problem is a key step in this 'input phase'.

The next phase is 'processing'. In this stage, it's important to relax your mind. Engage in stress-free activities, whether it's listening to music, practicing sports, or any other relaxing pastime. The goal is to minimize stress, as a relaxed mind is more adept at uncovering clear and positive solutions.

Finally, there's the 'output stage'. When your subconscious finds a solution, it communicates this through a sensation or feeling. The challenge is to recognize and interpret these signals, which might appear as indistinct images or thoughts in your mind. The next time you experience this, pause and reflect on these sensations. They may lead you to the answers you're seeking.

Developing Good Habits

Once you've gained the ability to influence your subconscious mind, the next step is to utilize this control to establish healthier habits. Our everyday behaviors and decisions are significantly influenced by our subconscious mind, serving as our internal guide and shaping our views and choices. Often operating as our 'instinct' or 'gut feeling', the subconscious is a powerful force in our lives.

Without proper guidance, our perceptions can become muddled by stress and other negative influences, leading to poor reactions. You can train your subconscious to adopt beneficial habits by focusing on concrete facts instead of subjective perceptions. It's crucial to remember that although you might not be able to alter the circumstances you face, you can change your emotional response to them.

Experts tell us that **90%** of the things we worry about will never happen to us. This insight highlights the need to focus on the actual root causes of our anxieties rather than simply our impressions of them. Here's how you can start:

1. First, ask yourself about the facts of the situation and as you write them down, try not to reflect on any emotions.

2. Second, ask yourself if there are alternative causes, rather than the one your subconscious is suggesting. Challenge your perception with evidence from other

sources that may falsify your perception.

3. Put perspective back into the situation by reflecting on the facts and alternative causes.

4. Challenge the perception you have had and create an alternative perception.

5. As you learn to challenge the way your subconscious relates to situations, you can manipulate it to start thinking positively. The goal is to challenge your subconscious reasoning before it *"thinks"* and responds negatively to situations.

"Affirmations are the building blocks of belief. Repeat them with conviction, and you'll construct a life you desire." - Barack Obama

How Subconscious Eating Can Affect Us?
Even with numerous challenges in life, the way you eat and your food choices are deeply affected by your subconscious. This is known as subconscious eating, where eating is more of an instinctive action than a conscious decision. For example, you might automatically start eating a food you like when it's offered to you, regardless of whether you're actually hungry. This habit can make it challenging to maintain or lose weight.A frequent error in subconscious thinking is to eat more when increasing physical activity. If the calories consumed are more than what's burnt off, weight loss won't happen; in fact, weight gain is more likely. To change eating habits, you must take a deliberate and active role. Consider a scenario where you want to go from 220 pounds to 121

pounds. Start by visualizing yourself at your goal weight, embedding a positive drive in your subconscious to control your eating and strive towards weight loss. Alongside watching your diet, exercise is key to achieving your goal. In the end, you hold complete power over your dietary choices, and blaming overeating on a lack of control is merely an excuse.

"The secret of change is to focus all of your energy not on fighting the old, but on building the new."

– Socrates

CHAPTER FOUR

BATTLING SHADOWS

THE POWER OF POSITIVITY

CHAPTER 4

BATTLING SHADOWS

"The silent promise of growth from within, nurturing resilience in the soil of the soul."

Within each person, there's a constant struggle between two forces, one representing darkness and the other light. These forces influence our viewpoints and decisions. The outcome depends on which force we nurture. However, we aren't just bystanders in this internal conflict between negative and positive thinking. Actively fostering a positive mindset can allow it to prevail. Reflect on your usual mindset - do you tend to be more pessimistic or optimistic? Neither is inherently right or wrong; each has its role. But while pessimism can lead to stress, optimism tends to be empowering. When faced with challenges, how do you respond?, pessimists often exaggerate obstacles and fear the worst, whereas optimists maintain hope, viewing difficulties as temporary and solvable. Often, our perspective is shaped by whether we see life as half-empty or half-full. However, this view oversimplifies the situation.

The reality is that you have the power to change how full your life's glass is. By owning your mindset, you have the ability to shift towards a more positive outlook. Embracing self-reliance is a crucial step in the journey of finding yourself, uninterrupted. It's important to move away from relying on others for approval, resources, or direction. Even though relying on each other is a natural part of being human, self-reliance offers the liberty and adaptability to shape your own path. Enhancing your problem-solving skills also nurtures a sense of optimism. Even amidst challenges, maintain the belief that you will eventually find a way out. Allow yourself the space to think of alternative solutions. Another important factor is to intentionally reduce time spent with consistently negative people. Allowing their pessimistic attitudes to influence you can distort your viewpoint. Be selective about whose opinions and attitudes you let affect you. Even the most optimistic people can find it hard to maintain positivity in tough times. In such moments, it's essential to consciously steer your thoughts towards more uplifting perspectives. Practicing gratitude is a good start. When frustration looms, take a moment to appreciate the good in your life – a safe home, a loving family, your health. Recognizing what you already have can help restore a balanced view. Recall instances when you've successfully overcome past challenges. These memories are a testament to your resilience and ability to navigate current obstacles. Keep in mind, you've overcome challenges in the past and you have the strength to succeed again. Laughter is another powerful tool to alleviate negative moods. Sharing humorous moments with positive people can ease stress and rekindle hope, thanks to the positive biochemical impact that laughter has on our mood.

If you find yourself losing a positive outlook in any situation, take charge of your emotions. Recognize that while you cannot control every event, your response remains in your hands, even in the toughest times. Most importantly, avoid exaggerating problems or viewing temporary issues as permanent. This mindset is key to maintaining a hopeful and balanced outlook.

Challenging situations and negative mindsets are not life sentences; they're just temporary pauses. Remember the timeless saying "this too shall pass." Developing a positive mindset involves retraining your mental habits, which have been shaped over a lifetime. There will be moments when maintaining an optimistic outlook seems unnatural. Stay determined through these times; with consistent practice, positivity will become your natural state.

As you develop these internal strengths - self-reliance, gratitude, humor, and owning your reactions - your vulnerability to outside negativity diminishes. You develop the means to protect your positive mindset from the invasive effects of pessimism. Strengthening this positive outlook enhances your ability to cope with hardships. This resilience grows stronger over time, creating an upward cycle that elevates you in the face of adversity. The benefits of ongoing optimism are not just mental but also physical. Positivity plays a key role in lowering stress and stress hormones, safeguarding against illness and boosting energy and motivation. Anticipating positive outcomes fosters choices rooted in confidence and a sense of abundance. Embracing healthy practices, such as balanced nutrition, sufficient sleep, consistent exercise, and surrounding yourself with uplifting individuals, becomes increasingly natural. As a result, negativity's influence on your decisions begins to diminish.

Over time, the hopeful world you picture transforms into your lived reality. The power of your thoughts in shaping your world is profound. While some may dismiss this as mere optimism, its impact is tangible. The direction of your focus determines where your energy flows. What you visualize, you draw into your life.

Your reality is a reflection of what's inside you. The mindset you adopt, therefore, shapes the course of your life. Why not choose positivity? This choice, which costs nothing, can bring significant benefits, unlocking your highest potential. You possess the means to feed and grow inherent positivity. Break free from the unnecessary limits of pessimism by training yourself to stay hopeful, no matter the situation. Navigate life's challenges with a consistent expectation of good outcomes. The most impactful decision we make each day is to live either in love or in fear. To choose an optimistic mindset is to believe that, regardless of circumstances, your life is rich with meaning, beauty, and possibilities. What perspective will you choose for your glass today?"

"Opportunities are often disguised as challenges. It's the optimist who unveils their true potential."
- Serena Williams

The Conflict Between Good And Bad

Optimism and pessimism represent two ends of a spectrum. When approaching any task, you engage with either a positive or negative viewpoint. Sometimes, you might have to take on tasks against your will. When this happens, try to view the task from a new perspective, focusing on its potential advantages. Adopting this approach can help you enjoy the task and begin with a positive mindset. A positive attitude generally leads to a more joyful state of mind, while a negative attitude can cause you to overlook the joys of life. One common yet unintentional habit is dwelling on past failures. To determine if you lean towards optimism or pessimism, listen to the voice of your heart. Reflect on how you've handled challenging situations in the past. What sort of thoughts came to your mind in those days? How did you manage the situation? Your responses to these reflections can reveal much about your general outlook on life.

"Optimism is the secret of self-reliance. Self-reliance is the secret of a dynamic power. A dynamic power is the secret of an immediate success" -Sri Chinmoy

Self-Reliance Is A Part Of Optimism
Every element in the world, whether living or nonliving, coexists in a harmonious relationship, mutually supporting and maintaining each other's existence. Plants, animals, and humans are interconnected and share life. We need each other, but being able to stand on our own is also important. This is true for everyone, everywhere. From the beginning, the importance of self-reliance is emphasized. In schools and colleges, children are taught the skills needed to navigate the complexities of life. They often face the challenge of adjusting to new environments on their own. But self-reliance is more than just financial independence; it involves thinking for oneself, putting in dedicated effort, and building confidence in one's abilities – all vital for achieving success. It's essential that young people learn this as they prepare for

their careers, understanding that education is not just about earning a livelihood but living a life of purpose. This philosophy resonates with Mahatma Gandhi's vision, where self-reliance is esteemed, and simplicity in work is celebrated as a mark of pride, not a reason for discomfort. It's about gracefully embracing one's independence and cherishing the honor that comes from being self-sufficient.

> *"Maintaining a positive outlook isn't just a choice; it's a catalyst for extraordinary change."*
> *- Ava DuVernay*

Stay Positive In Any Environment
Navigating through challenging situations is key to developing balanced self-reliance. Often, life places us in difficult environments, The best example to this is unemployment. Facing job loss can initially bring a wave of negativity. People's experiences vary: some quickly secure new jobs, while others may endure a prolonged job hunt. This can lead to frustration and a sense of despair, emotions that might inadvertently seep into job applications, potentially affecting an employer's decision. One effective method to stay positive in such times is to regularly reflect on the positive aspects of life. Writing down things like the support of loved ones, personal achievements, or even small daily victories can help cultivate a positive mindset. Additionally, engaging in enjoyable outdoor activities or hobbies can be a powerful antidote to pessimism. While it may initially seem daunting, actively participating in these activities can shift your mindset towards a more positive outlook. Investing time in your interests is not only fulfilling

but also a critical step in maintaining positivity in challenging times.

Stay Unaffected From Negative Thoughts Of People
Sometimes, despite your belief in overcoming negativity, it seems endless. Pessimists, are at every corner of the world, always looking forward to ruin your day. It's crucial to remain unaffected by their words. Here are some strategies to help you: When facing a challenging situation, negative-minded individuals often approach first, making discouraging remarks to instill fear. It's important not to internalize their comments. A polite response can help maintain your clarity and decision-making ability. Remember, taking things personally can be detrimental. Another approach is to respond to negativity with positivity. Challenging pessimistic individuals by countering their negativity with positive actions can undermine their confidence and prompt them to reconsider their behavior. Showing them the impact of their negativity, and maintaining your optimism, can potentially lead them to adjust their attitude. This approach highlights the strength of your positive outlook.

"Negativity is a thief of joy. Protect your happiness fiercely." - Iyanla Vanzant

Steps to Think Positively

Life inherently comes with its share of challenges and fluctuations. It is what it is. Advice about maintaining a positive outlook is common during tough times, but it's often easier said than done, especially when things aren't going as planned. Constant negativity can have detrimental effects on your health, so here are three effective techniques to maintain a positive mindset.

Start Your Day with Positivity: Each morning, begin with a dose of positivity. Engage with uplifting content, such as inspirational quotes or motivational speeches. This practice sets a positive tone for your day. In fact, going through the quotes in this book helps too! If reading isn't your preference, listening to uplifting talks can be equally beneficial.

Practice Positive Speech: The words you use, particularly those you speak to yourself, hold immense power. They shape how you perceive and react to situations. For instance, if you're stuck in traffic on your way to work, you have a choice: either to react negatively or to use the time in a positive way, like enjoying music. The choice of words and reaction can significantly alter your experience.

Embrace Total Responsibility: This might be challenging, but it's incredibly empowering. Acknowledging that your current life situation is a result of your past decisions, whether good or bad, grants you personal power. Accepting total responsibility creates personal power and because you always have a choice, you can change the course of your life if you so wish to! You just have to decide by exercising your responsibility on your life!

These strategies not only help in fostering a positive mindset but also empower you to take charge of your life and its outcomes.

"Change your thinking. Change your life! Your thoughts create your reality. Practice positive thinking. Act the way you want to be, and soon you will be the way you act" - Les Brown

Positive Thinking Can Change Your Life

Nowadays, many people seem more preoccupied with earning a living rather than creating a fulfilling life. There's a big difference: one outlook centers on what's lacking, while the other makes the most of what's already there. Focusing too much on making money, rather than enjoying life's experiences, can lead to stress and unhappiness.

A key strategy to manage life's pressures is through positive thinking. This involves an intentional focus on expecting favorable outcomes in various life aspects, including finances, health, and relationships. I can't stress it more. Concentrating on positive results fosters a sense of well-being and propels you forward, even in tough times.

But what if you naturally lean towards pessimism? Changing your mindset is possible, but it's not an overnight transformation. It requires time, patience, and commitment. Often, the biggest hurdle in this change is your own inner voice, which can sabotage your efforts if not managed effectively. The first step is to recognize and be aware of this inner dialogue. Understand that not everything you tell yourself is accurate. For instance, if contemplating a purchase that's financially stretching, instead of thinking, "It's too expensive," ask yourself, "How can I afford this?"

This shift prompts your mind to seek solutions, often leading to surprising and positive outcomes.

Positive Thinking And Its Effect On Health

We all know that feeling sad can lead to depression if it's not resolved. Studies have found that individuals who embrace positive thinking often suffer less from common illnesses, enjoy longer lifespans, and generally maintain better health. This link between emotional well-being and physical health, while not entirely understood, is undeniable. As people age physically, those who cultivate a positive mindset tend to retain a sense of youthfulness and confidence internally, along with higher energy levels. Optimism in life encourages us to make healthier choices in various aspects of our lives. People who are at ease and confident are more likely to have healthier eating habits, engage in regular exercise, and spend quality time with loved ones. These behaviors positively impact health and overall well-being. Essentially, it involves minimizing stress and maintaining a positive outlook, regardless of life's challenges. Prioritizing emotional health is crucial; regular self-assessment and proactive steps towards emotional wellness are key to a healthy lifestyle.

CHAPTER FIVE

SEED OF SELF-LOVE

WATERING THE ROOTS OF SELF-WORTH

CHAPTER 5

SEED OF SELF-LOVE

WATERING THE ROOTS OF SELF-WORTH

"Embrace self-love as the compass guiding you to unlock the mysteries of self-discovery."

Along life's journey, you'll inevitably encounter others whose behaviors annoy, frustrate or anger you. Their actions may seem totally unreasonable and even intentionally malicious. Yet how you respond determines whether these situations strengthen or weaken you. When people act in ways that irk you, start by asking what in their background or culture conditioned this conduct. We all absorb beliefs and habits from our developmental environments that seem perfectly normal and justified. Broadening your compassion reminds you of our shared humanity beneath divergent behaviors. Also examine your own triggers and where they originate. If you felt judged often as a child, you may project that dynamic onto others now. Their actions probably have little to do with you. What you react to strongest in others mirrors sensitivities within still needing healing.

Rather than lashing out defensively, breathe and create space between the frustrating behavior and your response. Take time to reflect so you can engage consciously rather than instinctively. Listen to understand their motivations and context. You'll gain insights about them and yourself to help diffuse the situation. When you do speak up, aim not to chastise them but to communicate how their actions impact you and others. Share how together you can find a resolution. They're more likely to listen if you speak your truth without attacking theirs. Find common ground. If no healthy resolution exists, you may need to limit contact with consistently difficult people. While total isolation is unwise, you needn't remain hostage to toxic patterns that sabotage your serenity. Be discerning about who and what you allow in your personal space. Life will inevitably bring criticisms and judgments from others. Hearing negative feedback activates our fight-flight-freeze responses, putting us on the defensive. But remember most people criticize out of their own unresolved pain, not because you deserve condemnation. When criticisms sting, avoid knee-jerk reactions. Take time to reflect on what truth may lie buried beneath the barbs before you respond. If the critique holds validity, be grateful for the opportunity to learn and improve. Offer sincere thanks for their honesty and care in wanting to see you grow.

Even untrue allegations, when received with equanimity, hold potential for soul growth. They remind us that all opinions ultimately reflect the speakers' perceptions, not objective reality. We get to choose what we accept as truth about us. Their distortions about you need not become your own. Criticisms urge us to embody our values consistently, to walk our talk. By taking the high road in these conversations, you model how to critique with compassion. Kill your enemies with kindness. Channel anger into empathetic understanding of their inner hurt. With love, even critics can become teachers. We cannot control others' behaviors but we have absolute authority over our responses. Keep the focus here. Bring consciousness to auto-reactions then intentionally choose higher-minded alternatives - dialogue over diatribe, education over belligerence, forgiveness over feuding. These enlightened choices break cycles poisoning your spirit.

Life delivers a mix of joy and adversity. Challenges arise to spur our growth, but without acceptance, they turn into unnecessary suffering. Serenity comes when we distinguish which aspects of life to change versus accept.

If faced with difficulties you can influence, summon the courage to take ownership. Avoid blaming people or circumstances. Victimhood disempowers whereas accountability liberates. Chart steps towards change one day at a time. Progress builds momentum. For situations beyond your control, strive to understand their deeper purpose. Explore how adapting your attitude could positively transform the circumstance. Even the darkest nights make the stars shine brighter. Each experience holds lessons to uplift you. Zoom out to discern whether your perspective of the problem needs adjusting. Viewing life's tapestry from a broader vantage point helps put trials into context. We endure storms but cannot steer the weather. Release needing specific outcomes. Peace resides in remembering all seasons eventually pass. Trust in life's larger rhythms. Ups and downs are equally purposeful. There are no failures, only feedback. Progress winds not in straight lines but forward nonetheless. Keep the faith. When conflicts arise with others, avoid attacking their position. Instead, validate what you can even in disagreeing. Seek first to understand their viewpoint before asking them to appreciate yours. Misunderstandings dissolve when both sides feel respected. Remember your truth is not the only truth. We inhabit shared space and must compromise. Listen earnestly, communicate thoughtfully, appeal to people's highest natures. Progress comes collaboratively, not combatively. Lead with light.

Self-Discovery Starts By Loving Yourself

Self-discovery is greatly dependent on whether you love yourself. Love for oneself is a great asset that one can have in life. First and foremost, you should ask yourself who you are *uninterrupted*. To a very large extent, most of us are deeply engrossed on the day-to-day hustles and bustles of life. This entails; making ends meet, running our various businesses and starting new paths for our careers. We are deeply engrossed in this until we forget who we really are. We never stop to discover ourselves. If you do not love yourself, then there's no way you can love somebody else. Always put yourself first and do not look down upon yourself. Loving yourself has nothing to do with ego; it does not mean looking down upon others or being too proud. There's no way you can love others if you do not love yourself first. Thus, loving yourself opens up your life to unique possibilities as you are comfortable in your own skin and is ready to take on anything that lies ahead.

Fall in Love with Yourself

Asking yourself, "Do I love myself?" Most people would probably evade the question, but it is an important and valid question which if we could all answer yes to, would change the way we feel about ourselves and give us self-confidence to achieve the dreams and desires we have for our lives. The feeling of being unloved and unworthy is isolating. If you struggle to identify aspects of yourself that you love, it's a sign that you need to work on self-love. Cultivating self-love is achievable. To love yourself you must challenge the negative feelings inside that center our thoughts. We must acknowledge that our self-worth and self- acceptance are about the person we are, the person we are comfortable being around when everyone else has left and when we are alone. We must realize by the end of the day, we are all we have. Take the time to sit and write all the things there is to love about yourself. Be honest with yourself. Do not let toxic thoughts hinder the process. Try to do these five simple things every day and you will find yourself thinking differently:

1. Write down positive qualities you possess and read them aloud to yourself often.

2. Learn to self-care and do something every day that you enjoy. You deserve it!

3. Look at yourself in the mirror, appreciate the person you see, and affirm their worth and reasons for being

loved every day.

4. Fill your life with people who love you and tell you
    often what a special person you are. Accept their words
    and their love without questioning it.

Embracing positive affirmations about yourself naturally
leads to a deeper love for who you are, and prepares you to
confidently tackle any upcoming challenges.

*"I wake up every morning believing today is
going to be better than yesterday." - Will Smith*

Everyday Another Gift
Each morning when you awaken, it's like experiencing a
rebirth. You're presented with a fresh opportunity to shape
your life as you see fit. Reflect on this: every breath signifies
life, and with life comes the power to alter your path. The
freedom of choice is always yours; you're never compelled to
follow a set path. Each moment of your existence offers a
chance, a decision point. This means that every day presents
you with 86,400 opportunities to reinvent yourself and
redirect your life's journey. The real power lies in making a
decisive choice at any given moment. To help you harness
this power of decision-making, I'd like to introduce you to the
Countdown method. This technique is a tested approach that
helps you make sharp, focused decisions, effectively
strengthening your decision-making abilities.

How Does This Work?

Simple. The next time you feel as if you can't decide or you don't know what you want. Countdown from 4...,3...,2...,1...and decide. It's that simple. Follow you gut feel and decide. This is effective because it eliminates over thinking and paralysis through analysis.

> *"Success is liking yourself, liking what you do, and liking how you do it." - Maya Angelou*

Know What Makes You Happy

Do you know what makes you happy?

If you do then you have discovered true gold. This isn't about the fleeting joy that comes from indulging in a favorite dessert or driving a luxurious car. Such pleasures are temporary; once the dessert is gone or the car is returned, the same issues that clouded your happiness may resurface. The happiness referred to here is a deeper, enduring kind, one that offers solace and keeps you at peace with yourself and the world, regardless of external circumstances.

For some, happiness is rooted in their spiritual relationship with God. Others find joy in new hobbies or sports, or in fulfilling different roles in their life. But are these the true sources of lasting happiness?

The cornerstone of enduring happiness is self-acceptance. It's this acceptance that equips us to navigate life's challenges. While we may express self-acceptance in our spiritual life or relationships, it's only when we accept ourselves that we find true contentment. Psychologists have long emphasized the importance of the relationship we have with ourselves. Even when life hits us hard, its impact is lessened if we have cultivated a deep love for ourselves. This self-love, recognizing our own worth as 'true gold,' is where real happiness lies. In self-acceptance, we find a haven, understanding that our identity isn't shaped by our experiences. Instead, we shape our experiences through our responses to them.

You Are Worth It!

Do you feel you are not good enough?

Everything you do feels like it eventually amounts to nothing so you don't even try? You find yourself spinning in a downwards spiral because you feel like you don't measure up? For those who feel this way, this might be their "reality" or truth. Research has shown that the feeling of unworthiness is one of the common contributing factors of weight gain and emotional eating disorders. We all have room to grow and develop and the most liberating truth of all is that each of us is unique and beautiful. There is no one quite like you on this earth and there never will be. Once we accept this, we can then focus on ways to improve ourselves. Without appreciating this perspective, it feels as if we are constantly striving to find self-acceptance externally instead of willingly and wholeheartedly accepting ourselves for who we are. This creates an unhealthy dependency on external validation. A person who only feels happy when people praise him or her will never genuinely feel happy because external praises will die down and is not long lasting. People can't be praising us 24 hours, 7 days a week. An old African proverb reminds us if there are no enemies within, then no external enemies can cause us harm or hurt. This means that if we are at peace with ourselves then whatever events or occurrences that are perceived to be bad and negative will not affect us unless we allow it to. So I want you to challenge those thoughts. Starting tomorrow choose one action to do for you yourself. It could be as simple as taking that trip to the beach which you have always wanted to or buying that shirt which makes you look good. Give yourself a gift just because. It doesn't need to be fancy if you don't want it to but you MUST feel the genuine feeling of giving yourself a gift and rewarding yourself. Thank yourself for bring you this far in life regardless of the outcome because you know what?

* **You're still alive!**
Most people struggle with self-sabotage and often fail to speak kindly of themselves, but you stand apart from the crowd – a key reason you've chosen this book. You're on a mission to discover who you are, *uninterrupted*. You're committed to self-improvement, so approach this journey with the seriousness it deserves. Remember, you are absolutely worth this effort.

"It is so liberating to really know what I want, what truly makes me happy, what I will not tolerate. I have learned that it is no one else's job to take care of me but me." - Beyoncé

Expect Good Things To Happen In Your Life
Studies shows that expecting positive outcomes in our lives often leads them to materialize. While being positive doesn't automatically ensure success, there's a clear connection between positive anticipation and the release of endorphins

in our brain. These endorphins, acting as natural pain relievers, assist us in managing stress and facing challenges with a clearer mind, enabling us to find solutions more effectively. On the other hand, having low or negative expectations can block the release of endorphins. This can lead to increased feelings of depression, making it harder to think positively or envision good outcomes in tough situations. If negative thinking persists, it can become a habitual mindset, which is difficult to break without significant effort. The expectations set by others around us, such as teachers and parents, also shape our own. Positive expectations from them can inspire and motivate, leading to improved performance. Conversely, negative expectations can contribute to self-doubt and a focus on poor outcomes.

A person driven by high self-expectations and a clear vision for their goals will actively seek ways to realize their dreams. This pursuit itself generates endorphins, aiding in maintaining focus despite obstacles. Each small success further fuels positive expectations and outcomes. In contrast, someone lacking motivation and plagued by self-doubt may fixate on negative prospects, leading to a cycle of self-sabotage. If you find yourself in a cycle of low self-expectation and negative thinking, it's beneficial to surround yourself with positive, supportive people. They can help you refocus and rebuild your belief in yourself and your aspirations. The critical question to reflect on is: do you expect good things to happen in your life?"

"I am my best work - a series of road maps, reports, recipes, doodles, and prayers from the front lines." - Audre Lorde

Love Among People Leads To A Happy Life
In the universe, love stands as the most profound emotion.
When guided by love, everything seems within reach and the
world glows brighter. The opposite of love is not hate but
fear. Fear restricts us, creating a sense of lack and limitation.
Love on the other hand, brings courage, determination,
understanding, and a host of positive feelings. When love is
present among people regardless of race or background,
there is understanding, harmony, and advancement. Fear,
however, leads to conflict and violence. Often driven by the
unknown, of being threatened and of unrealistic fear.
Imagine a world where love is the primary driving force in
everyone's life. In such a world, disputes and separations
among couples would be rare. Harmony would replace
tension between parents and children, friendships would be
free of bitterness, and the exploitation of one person by
another would be non-existent.

*"As we express our gratitude, we must never forget that
the highest appreciation is not to utter words, but to
live by them" - John F. Kennedy*

What Makes You Feel Loved?
What actions by others make you feel cherished? Is it
receiving thoughtful gifts or heartfelt notes and messages
assuring you that you are loved and appreciated?
Maybe you are the type of person who appreciates a hug as a
way of feeling loved, or really enjoy spending time with your
spouse or best friend. The ways we express love often mirror
our own desires for affection. Many couples find joy in
showing love to each other. Yet, there's an important
realization to grasp: the way we feel loved might differ from

how others perceive and express love. Understanding what makes your partner or children feel loved is essential for nurturing deep, passionate relationships. While hearing "I love you" is comforting, for some, words alone are insufficient. Saying you love someone without aligning your actions to their love language can lead to confusion and worry, even in strong relationships. Discovering what makes you feel loved and learning what your loved ones need to feel cherished is a journey of personal growth that can enhance your relationships. It's a simple skill to acquire and, when applied, can profoundly transform your relationships.

> *"Don't be pushed around by the fears in your mind. Be led by the dreams in your heart."*
> *- Roy T. Bennett*

Make It Beautiful

Today's fast-paced world often sees people rushing and competing with each other. In this race, there are winners and losers, leading to feelings of joy or disappointment. Just as the sun brings light to one part of the world while the other remains in darkness, life too is a mix of joy and sorrow. Life, like a boat on a stormy ocean, doesn't always sail smoothly. Recognizing life's struggles is essential to appreciating its joys. Some people focus only on life's hardships, overlooking past happiness and the likelihood of its return. The essence of life is the coexistence of joy and sorrow; each gives meaning to the other. Life's challenges act as a protective barrier around moments of happiness. The English poet Shelley once said, "Our sweetest songs are those that tell of saddest thought." Life's story is made up of both comedy and tragedy, each adding depth and character to our experiences. Joy and sorrow should be faced calmly, as taught in various scriptures. We shouldn't become overly joyous in success or give in to feelings of hopelessness during difficult times. History's greatest figures have all navigated the pleasures and pains.

"I've learned over the years that people are human and have mood swings, regardless of how talented they are. Today, I'm looking at life from a realistic point of view instead of the way I would want things to be"
- Otis Williams

Improve Your Mood Swings

Do you ever feel frustrated with yourself for being irritable and moody with your loved ones? Understanding our emotional fluctuations and the impact of hormones and stress responses can be helpful. But it's important to realize that our moodiness is frequently influenced by factors we can manage. Recognizing and mitigating these influences can lead to a more positive and composed demeanor, improving our interactions both at home and in the workplace.

1. **If we don't get enough sleep, we will become moody.** Every adult should ideally have between 6 and 8 hours of sleep each night. Most people need at least 7 hours sleep, yet usually we find the time we have available for sleeping is getting lesser as our lives become busier. Increasing the amount of sleep will help us control our mood swings

.

2. **Check your diet. Ensure you are eating a balanced diet** that includes plenty of vegetables and fruit, grains and nuts, protein sources and carbohydrates. Cortisol, a steroid hormone is produced when we are thirsty or hungry and this hormone reduces the immune system and increases our feeling of stress. It is easily reduced by eating and drinking and accounts for the feeling of well-being many obese emotional eaters feel when they eat.

3. **Engage in a whole brain activity, such as a sport** or other fitness activity to improve your feeling of well-being and reduce your stress levels. These activities have been shown to improve emotions, logic and ability to learn. This explains why women attending a gym regularly describe feelings of euphoria at the end of their work out session.

4. **Too much television and computer time can affect your moods.** The addictive nature of television and computers can create tension and anxiety when they need to be turned off or is interrupted, regardless if how important the reason.

5. **You yourself can be the cause of your mood swings.** Author Jeff Conley once said*"we must take a checkup from the neck up"* When we are feeling stressed or upset, we should try to minimize the damage by tuning up ourselves and our families and seeking to create a harmonious home for our families.

CHAPTER SIX

FINDING BALANCE

THE WELL OF RESILIENCE

CHAPTER 6

FINDING BALANCE

THE WELL OF RESILIENCE

"Life's journey is a canvas of limitless possibilities. Paint it intentionally with your dreams, priorities, and daily choices.

Life's journey offers boundless potential for joy, adventure and growth. Yet we must take ownership of our path to access this abundant fullness. Design your days with intention to create a life aligned with your truth.
Begin by clarifying your priorities. What contributions do you want to make? What relationships, pursuits and qualities are most important to you? Envision your best life in vivid detail. These visions become the compass guiding your daily decisions. With intention as your North Star, assess how you currently spend your hours and energy. Do your typical rhythms and habits support your dreams and values? If not,

what needs recalibrating? Start keeping a journal to track your days. Note moments that energize you versus those depleting your vitality.. See clearly how you invest your irreplaceable time. Knowledge is power to shift what is not working. Now create a blueprint for your ideal week. Schedule priorities that feel life-giving while still balancing must-dos. Protect time for self-care, passions and loved ones as jealously as you guard work obligations. At first this restructuring may feel uncomfortable. Old patterns do not relinquish their hold easily. But staying the course builds new neural pathways that become familiar in turn. With consistency, inspired living grows into a habit. While plotting your days thoughtfully, remain open to spontaneity. The most precious moments happen accidentally when we greet them with presence. Avoid over-regimentation; leave space for magic. Life dances between structure and flow. Along the way, you'll inevitably encounter tasks or asks in opposition to your priorities. Decline judiciously to protect your intentions while also hearing 'no' gracefully when others cannot accommodate your requests. 'No' need not be selfish or callous but an act of alchemy, transforming duty into freedom. Wield this power unapologetically. As your outer life reshapes to align with your inner truth, you may experience growing pains. Birth pangs of the emerging new you. Upheaval signals breakthrough. Trust in your higher guidance, even when the mind cries danger. Your soul navigates by stars invisible to your fears. Leap. In this reorientation process, anchor in practices that reconnect you with stillness beneath the churning. Meditation, yoga, breath work, prayer, journaling - choose those that resonate most and weave these lifelines into daily rhythms. No matter how chaotic the surface, serenity lives at your core. Drink from

that well. You possess inherent wisdom to walk your unique
path with courage and joy if you take time to listen inward.
By consistently tuning out the static to hear your inner voice,
your choices become mapped by your soul's luminous insight.
This inner light always guides you towards your highest
good, even when that means leaving behind the familiar.
Remember expansion lies beyond comfort zones. Be willing
to dwell in ambiguity during transitions between chapters.
Breathe through fear. The other side holds wonders
unimagined. As your vision clarifies and your actions align
with your intentions, your life transforms into a vibrant
reflection of your soul. Passion projects launch. Creative
expression flows. You feel called to your rightful place.
Keep surveying your path to ensure it remains true. We all get
distracted by detours diverging from our purpose. When you
feel lost or depleted, return to practices that reconnect and
replenish you. Find your way back through presence.
You hold dominion over your existence. With courage and
consciousness, build days that resonate. Keep releasing and
revising so your life continues unfolding into an ever-fuller
expression of your highest potentials. The seeds of your
destiny live within you. Water them with self-care, prune
them with discipline, nurture them with faith. Harvests
beyond your wildest dreams will bloom.

*"The greatest weapon against stress is our ability to
choose one thought over another" - William James*

Time Out For Self-Renewal And Self-Development
Taking a break is a chance for solitude, focused on personal growth and reflecting who you are uninterrupted. It's incredibly rewarding. When did you last indulge in a quiet evening alone or a brief getaway?
Sadly, many people skip such breaks. Why? The reasons vary: family responsibilities, demanding work schedules, or simply a lack of time. However, allowing yourself this pause is a form of self-rejuvenation. It's a time to clear your mind and concentrate on your goals.
Let's explore the advantages of prioritizing this practice at least once a year;

1. Taking extended time out gives you the chance to take a step back and decide how to move forward in your life. When you are in the middle of life and all its responsibilities, it's easier to focus on survival and not on achievement. Take the time out each year to achieve some life goals.

2. Time out is not a selfish activity, but a time to be critical and honest about yourself and your life. The focus is to improve your relationships and to help your family and friends. It gives you the opportunity to evaluate what you are doing currently and how you can improve it.

3. Taking a few hours or a few days out of your busy schedule is not running away from your responsibilities. Rather, it is an opportunity to develop a new enthusiasm so you can keep "running towards them".

Most people are keen to take the time out but struggle with how to achieve it. Here are some suggestions:

1. Discuss with your partner. Decide on taking the time out together or individually. If children are involved, try to get the help of grandparents, siblings or friends.

2. If you are doing it with a partner, try to schedule alone time during your retreat as well as time together.

Once you have scheduled a time out, it is essential to plan on how to make the most from it. Preparing for the journey is as important as being there. Here are some suggested ways to prepare for your time out experience:

1. Choose a location that will help you to relax. Whether or not it is close to home, the key is to relax and refresh.

2. Don't bring anything that will act as a distraction. If you take your cell phone with you, try to borrow one that does not allow you to be tempted to check email or spend time on the Internet.

3. You can take a personal tape recorder or a journal to enable you to record your reflections and goals as you create them.

4.   If religion is important to you, take a religious book or self-help manual if you would like to use them as part of your meditation.

When you arrive at your time out location and begin the process of self-reflection, here are some guidelines to help you focus:

1.   Evaluate what caused you to feel sad and happy as you review your life. These will help you to focus on things that need addressing in your life.

2.   Celebrate the things you have achieved, and goals you have accomplished.

3.   Create action plans for those things you feel sad or dissatisfied with.

"I've learned it's important not to limit yourself. You can do whatever you really love to do, no matter what it is" - Ryan Gosling

It's Not What You Can't Do, But What You Can
Do you often dwell on your limitations and feel regret for not being able to achieve certain things? Or do you wish to improve in activities you enjoy? Many of us experience these thoughts and handle them differently. Instead of fixating on what you can't do, try to concentrate on your abilities and enhance them. Perfecting our skills boosts our self-esteem. It's common to have conflicting inner dialogues. Even when others compliment us, we might struggle to accept it without self-deprecation. Our inner critic often overpowers others'

positive words. By focusing on our strengths, we can increase our self-confidence. This week, take time to celebrate your talents, especially those you excel at. Seek input from your partner or friends to identify your strong points. Dedicate your efforts to turning your skills into excellence and take pride in your accomplishments. Learn to accept and relish praise for your achievements.

"You only live once, but if you do it right, once is enough" - Mae West

It Is Your Life! Embrace It
Reflect on your current life situation. Are you where you aspire to be? Consider your personal relationships, habits, financial status, spiritual health, and career. These aspects profoundly influence how you perceive yourself without any interruptions. It's crucial to remember that if you don't steer the course of your life, someone or something else will take control of it for you. As children, we were often asked, "What do you want to be when you grow up?" Teenagers fantasize about ideal relationships, and young adults make plans for exciting international trips. As we grow older, it's vital to reignite these aspirations and dreams. Why not conduct a thorough review of your life, noting down goals in every significant area? Explore the internet or visit your local library to find resources for acquiring new skills or knowledge in the fields you wish to develop.

Ask yourself these questions:

1. What are my goals and dreams?

2. How do my goals and dreams fit into the circumstances of my life at this moment?

3. What areas do I need training in to achieve my goals?

4. Who will be the best source of advice to take control of areas that are out of control now?

5. Where can I find resources to help me achieve my goals and if I can't find any myself?

6. Where can I go to find the information I need in order to start my progress towards achieving them?

7. What things in my life need to change so I have time to achieve my goals?

8. What attitudes in my life need to change so I have the intention to achieve my goals?

9. With whom can I share these goals with so that I have someone to be my cheerleader as I embrace my goals?

Each of these questions help you to prepare insights into yourself, your ambitions and goals to create a practical way to work towards achieving them and embracing the life you want for yourself and your family.

"Life is better when you do what makes you happy regardless of what others think. It's your life, not theirs" - Sonya Parker

What Makes You Happy?

Consider what truly brings you joy. In our daily quest for happiness, are we truly discovering it, or are we chasing an elusive dream? Some find their joy in accumulating wealth or possessions, while others seek it in relationships with spouses, partners, or children. Many women engage in shopping as a form of seeking joy. For some, the delight may come from a luxurious box of chocolates. Men, too, often find their pleasure in social gatherings or weekend sports. Our pursuit of happiness is relentless, even if it's fleeting. Yet, relying on others, indulging in treats, or acquiring more things often leads to temporary satisfaction. True happiness isn't found in external sources. Enduring satisfaction comes from finding peace and fulfillment within ourselves and appreciating our daily lives.

Here are some thoughts that will help you discover how to be content and achieve happiness:

1. **Don't spend money to find happiness:** You will never be happy if you think money can buy happiness, or that happiness lies in possessions. It just leads to discontentment.

2. **Don't worry about the future:** Your happiness is available to you today. Many people live in hopes that tomorrow they will be happy. Expect happiness to be

yours today!

3. **Find your happiness in believing:** Life without belief is a life without hope.

4. **Look at others who are in a worse situation than you and be thankful for what you have**: Contentment and gratitude are the easiest paths to inner happiness.

5. **You need to want to be happy**: Someone wisely said once *"Who does not want to be happy"*

6. **Help Others:** Their pleasure and appreciation will increase your own happiness!

"Don't worry, be happy..." True happiness lies in those four small words. Being happy is a choice, not a pursuit!

"Smile at strangers and you just might change a life." - Steve Maraboli

A Smile Can Change Everything

When we are worrying about something, it usually shows on our face, betraying the calm demeanor we try to maintain. Smiling is often the last thing we feel like doing, particularly in the darkest of times. However, choosing to smile through our struggles can unlock an energizing force that eases some of our burdens.

It's often said *"Smiling is a social obligation."* Think of the times a stranger's smile has lifted your spirits, leading you to respond with a smile of your own and a surge of optimism. Smiling triggers the release of a hormone in our brain that improves our mood and outlook, making us feel happier. This effect can spread, as smiles tend to be returned by those we encounter. During stress, many prefer to stay home and avoid social interactions. Yet, it's beneficial to connect with family and friends and not withdraw into solitude. When alone, engage in activities that induce laughter, like reading a humorous book or watching a comedy. Laughter stimulates a positive reaction in our brain.

Combat negative emotions by focusing on joyful and inspiring activities. Being around cheerful people and in fun environments can positively affect your mindset, as the optimism of others can be infectious.

"Life is not measured by the number of breaths we take, but by the moments that take our breath away." - Maya Angelou

Think Happy Thoughts And Learn To Fly

Peter Pan was asked by his friend Wendy on how she can fly like him. He replied that to fly, all she had to do was to think happy thoughts. Although Peter Pan and Wendy are characters of fiction, the essence of this story carries a profound truth. Joyful thoughts might not grant us the power of flight, but they certainly have the power to uplift our spirits.

This story illuminates a common misconception about happiness. Often, people let their life situations dictate their mood, with their happiness fluctuating based on external events. However, This shouldn't be the case. Every day presents an opportunity to cultivate our happiness, which is more an attitude than a mere response to life's events. There are practical strategies that can be adopted to nurture genuine happiness. These habits can easily become part of your daily life, turning happiness from a fleeting emotion into a constant state of being.

1. **Help other people.**
    As long as your focus is always on yourself, you are aware of things that are not as good as they could be in your life.

2. **Find something to be thankful for every day.**
    Look around your world every day and find at least one thing to be thankful about each day. Write it down in a journal and review your journal regularly to help you remember the good things in your life.

3. **Surround yourself with good friends.**
    Happiness is contagious as you should have known by now. As you surround yourself with happy people who are positive, their happiness will affect you and your happiness will affect them. =) - Peter Pan

4. **Head down memory lane regularly.**
    Your life is full of happy memories. Write down why those things made you happy and laugh with someone who remembers them often.

5. **Nurture those you love.**
    "How much time do you invest into improving your marriage, or developing your parenting skills?" Research shows that the happiest people are those with the strongest relationships with their significant others.

6. **Look after your health.**
    Enjoy yourself running around with the children, doing Zumba at the gym or playing golf with your mates. Looking after your health fills you with energy and when you add laughter to the fun you are the winner!

7. **Try something new you have always wanted to do.**
    Set yourself a challenge to do something new every week no matter how much you feel you can't do it. Have a go and enjoy the experience. You may find yourself surprised by the results.

8. **Don't expect too much.**
    Keep your expectations on yourself and others at a reasonable level. If you set the standard too high, you are setting yourself for disappointment. Accept and appreciate the things that people do for you.

Happiness is in our reach if we focus on achieving it. Appreciate the good things in our life and the gift of love that is given to us by our significant others. They are the things that remain constant when other things in our life are not going as well. They help us keep the difficult moments we will inevitably face in perspective and give us hope when things around us may seem hopeless.

Is Lack of Happiness Robbing You Of Real Happiness?
Do you ever feel like life has shortchanged you, leaving you without the joy and peace you deserve? This could stem from various challenges, like financial struggles, relationship problems, or chronic health issues. It's important to realize that everyone, regardless of their wealth, fame, or success, faces tough times and feels that life has handed them a challenging set of issues. However, many people manage to smile through their struggles by focusing on the positive aspects of their lives rather than dwelling on the negatives. The key to finding true happiness is in appreciating life's blessings rather than dwelling on its imperfections. Remember, each individual is shaped by their unique past experiences, and conflicts are inevitable in human interactions. By focusing on the positives in others and the benefits of our relationships, we gain a fresh perspective on appreciation, even in challenging situations.
While some differences may be too great to overcome, true happiness often differs from what we perceive it to be. Constantly comparing our lives and relationships to those of others can be detrimental. As we embrace this essential life lesson, we open ourselves to discovering happiness in unexpected places.

What Have You Gifted Yourself Today?

Depending on which culture you were brought up in, you may be raised to be a good giver or a good receiver. In many African cultures, such as those in Ghana or Kenya, there's a strong emphasis on contributing to the community and placing group needs over personal desires. But being a good giver without being an equally good receiver can create imbalance. You might miss out on the joy of receiving. To check if you're not great at receiving, reflect on how you treat yourself. Have you recently indulged in something you truly desire? How do you respond to compliments - do you dismiss them or accept them with grace? Failing to receive can block the flow of joy and miracles in your life. The universe is eager to give, but you need to be ready to accept its gifts.

Start changing this by embracing compliments wholeheartedly. Treat yourself to something you've longed for and revel in it. By receiving more, you'll be in a stronger position to give, because you can only share what you have. So, focus on filling your own cup first!

CHAPTER SEVEN

GUIDING LIGHT

DIVINE TIMING

CHAPTER 7

GUIDING LIGHT

DIVINE TIMING

"Release limiting beliefs, and let your radiant light guide not only yourself but also those who seek their own brilliance."

Everything you require to realize your soul's fullest expression already lives within you. But limiting beliefs often obscure your inner light. By releasing these constraints, your gifts can shine. We each possess a unique genius - an amalgam of talents, quirks, passions and sensibilities unlike any other. Like Michelangelo freeing sculptures from stone, self-discovery chips away all that is not you to reveal the masterpiece beneath. What dream, if realized, would bring you aliveness? What problem in the world inspires you to solve it? Your purpose is unveiled in the intersection of your innate talents and the world's needs. Identify these coordinates to chart your course. Commit to know yourself deeply. Keep excavating layers, dismantling outdated conditioning and stories. Mental clutter distorts your lens; clean it to see clearly. You glean wisdom from both light and shadow if you invite all parts of you into the light without judgement. Observe the push and pull between your inner voices. The affirming angel on one shoulder, the critic on the other. Thank both for trying to protect you, then empower your highest self to lead. You know your truth. Monitor when your energy depletes and when it charges. These clues reveal where you stray from your essence. Realign with activities, people and environments that make your soul soar. Your spirit knows its native habitat. If fears constrain you, name them to tame them. Look beneath the surface. Are you avoiding risk or embracing growth? Both elicit discomfort but only one leads to freedom. Leap, and the net appears. You were made for more. In stillness, beyond the mind's commotion, your inner voice emerges. Learn its language, subtle and symbolic. Synchronize each choice with its promptings. This inner compass points unwaveringly to your joy. When faced with decisions, retreat into meditation. The answers you seek unveil themselves when you quiet the mind chatter. Solutions arise from silence within. Keep refining your vision of your highest self. With dedicated focus, your inner image materializes externally. Thoughts compose the score that life dances to. Concentrate yours intentionally. You are the alchemist transmuting base metals into gold, carving your sovereignty from circumstance. But mastery requires diligence. Distraction is the enemy of visionaries. Stay vigilant. Your future self is calling you home. Each day offers opportunities for soul growth. The people and events arriving on your path do so at divine timing to catalyze your unfolding. Greet all with openness. Difficulties strengthen you when you lean in to their lessons. Be eager to evolve. When old fears or falsehoods reappear, greet them with compassion for the hurt parts of you still needing love. Then consciously recommit to your joy and worth. You are safe to shine. Give permission to your radiance. The more you know and express your authentic nature, the more you magnetize your soul tribe - those who see, nurture and celebrate your light. You find home in beloved community. You were never meant to walk alone. As you actualize your gifts, you inspire others to become fully themselves. Your purpose is activated by empowering people to own their power, just as you have. Each soul awakened brightens the collective. You change the world by healing yourself. This lifelong journey of self-discovery leads ever inward and upward, polishing your soul's illumination. But the wise understand that to soar, first you must let go. Release all that dims your light. You were born to fly. Trust in your wings.

"Don't let the behavior of others destroy your inner peace" - Dalai Lama

Handling Others' Irritating Behaviors

Each of us carries a unique set of principles shaping our views and feelings about life, including what we deem right or wrong. When others act outside our boundaries of acceptable behavior, we usually react in a negative way. Understanding that what seems incorrect to us might not be the same for others is an important part of personal growth. While we might disagree with their choices, we learn to respect and allow others to express their true selves. They possess different values and beliefs. Our reactions are often rooted in our upbringing; for instance, we're taught to chew with our mouths closed. This practice becomes significant to us and our family standards. So, encountering people who haven't been taught similar manners can naturally lead to frustration. Our own values and manners often become a yardstick for judging others. While we can't always control our initial reactions to different behaviors, we can learn to modify our perceptions and responses to them.

"If you want to fly, you have to give up the things that weigh you down." - Toni Morrison

Dealing With Criticism

"If you keep your head when all about you are losing theirs and blaming it on you" is a line from Rudyard Kipling's famous poem *"If."* There are probably many of us who can identify with the words and understand the frustration of being misunderstood or unfairly judged. It's a common experience for us or our loved ones to face such situations regularly. According to the poem, the way we react to these instances reflects our maturity and character. Learning to handle criticism and negative remarks is a sign of emotional growth. Criticism often feels like an attack on our self-esteem, prompting a defensive reaction to shield ourselves from discomfort. We might find ourselves apologizing for our actions or those of others, or even shifting the blame. So what are some of the positive ways we can respond to criticism?

1. Look at the incident as an opportunity for learning and self-growth and not as an attack on your self-esteem.

2. Much of the anger that eventuates from criticism has the risk of becoming a grudge. So always make an effort to forgive the person. Actively seek to work with them to negotiate a solution you are both satisfied with.

3. Try to take a step back before you respond. Thank them for their words and tell them you will consider and discuss it with them on another occasion. This approach enables both of you to calm and rationalize your actions further.

4. Think about the criticism; ask yourself if it is justified. If it is, then seek ways to prevent the situation from recurring and, if it is not, take steps to refute it calmly and preferably with evidence.

5. Don't dwell on the criticism but move on. Your value is not determined by one piece of criticism!

"Life is meant to be a challenge, because challenges make you grow" - Manny Pacquiao

Facing Life Challenges

Do you ever feel like your life is veering off course and spiraling out of control? In such moments, we're faced with two options. We can either acknowledge that there are aspects of our lives we can't alter, or focus on those we can change. When change is within our reach, it's crucial not to just wait for things to improve but to actively work towards making those changes. Often, we're aware of the need for change in our lives but delay taking action to better our situation. Leaving things as they are can lead to them dominating our lives. Francis of Assisi sought the "courage to change the things that can be changed, accept the things that can't, and the wisdom to know the difference." This prayer highlights the importance of discerning between changeable and unchangeable aspects of our lives. It's the first step in addressing a negative situation. We must consider whether the situation is changeable and, if so, identify actionable steps to enact that change.

Once we've established whether change is possible and how to implement it, we need to take action. If change is deemed impossible, it's important to view the situation in a broader context. Accepting that some problems are permanent, we should focus on minimizing their impact and appreciating the aspects of our life that remain unaffected by these issues.

Zoom In On Your Life

Imagine capturing a snapshot of your life today and then zooming in on a meaningful or significant aspect. Which part of your existence would you highlight? Is it a source of stress or joy? If your still image transformed into a film, what title would you assign it? Do you embrace this experience or wish it had never unfolded? Would you relive this chapter of your life if given the chance, and if not, why? Viewing our lives through the lens of a movie or photograph offers a deeper introspection. By naming pivotal life moments, we can concentrate on the impactful events shaping our present. Consider how a wide-angled shot captures much scenery but little detail. Zooming in on an intriguing part means missing the broader view. This mirrors how we often perceive life, appreciating the grand scheme but overlooking the nuances that add beauty and intrigue. A singular viewpoint risks losing diverse perspectives. We require these varied angles to grasp the essence and purpose of our life experiences. Reexamine your photographic memory. Observe the differences when viewed up close versus from afar.

If the close-up view is troubling, try stepping back for a wider perspective. How does this alter your perception?

Thus, focusing solely on the broader aspects of life may lead us to neglect the unique and smaller elements that individualize our existence.

"Hate is too great a burden to bear. It injures the hater more than it injures the hated." - Coretta Scott King

Respecting Different Views

When presented with different opinions, many people tend to defend their own viewpoints, which can be perceived as a challenge to others' beliefs. This often leads to unnecessary confrontations and strains personal and professional relationships. So how can we present our point of view without creating this reaction in people?. The key is empathy: understanding the situation from the other person's viewpoint as well as our own. This approach allows us to communicate our thoughts and feelings effectively, typically leading to more constructive outcomes.

This technique is an excellent way to approach all communications, be it with family, friends, colleagues, or acquaintances. It involves not just expressing our own thoughts and opinions but also acknowledging the legitimacy of the other person's perspective. By doing so, we communicate respect for their opinions and feelings, even during disagreements. This method doesn't necessarily mean agreeing with both viewpoints as equally valid, but it does respect the right of each person to their perspective. It's about valuing the relationship more than the specific issue at hand. As the saying goes, "to understand someone, walk a mile in their shoes." By considering their perspective, we shift from an "I want" approach to a more inclusive "I understand your feelings, may I offer another viewpoint?" attitude. Adopting this technique helps us learn an essential life skill: fostering and maintaining relationships despite disagreements. It equips us to handle potential conflicts in a way that encourages dialogue and resolution, rather than confrontation.

"There is no such thing as work-life balance -it is all life. The balance has to be within you" - Sadhguru

Achieving Life Balance

Many of us have aspirations and obligations in our lives. You might desire to exercise more or read more books this year. Do you, like many others, often wish for more time to pursue these interests? While managing time is crucial for these goals, there are preliminary steps to consider. Documenting these steps in a journal, as you explore and understand your personal needs, can guide you towards a balance between work and personal life. This balance is key to accomplishing the things you aspire to do at this stage of your life *uninterrupted.*

1. **List Your Goals**

   All of us have goals that change regularly and that reflect other things going on in our life at the time. List your goals and prioritize them from important to least important. Include not only the goals you have to achieve, but also the personal goals you want to achieve.

2. **List Your Daily Schedule**
    Although we want more time in the day, all of us have
    24 hours. We use some of these hours for sleep and
    some of these for work and recreation purposes. List
    down your daily schedule and include the things you
    must do because they are a commitment. This may
    include work commitments or school sport
    commitments with the children.

3. **Prioritize Your Personal Goals with Equal Priority as
    Work Related Goals**
    Don't minimize the time available to do the things you
    want to do, particularly if they are contributing to your
    life goals or well being. Include family time and other
    essential life activities that require your time and
    attention.

4. **Keep to the schedule unless it is an emergency**
    Most people who create a daily schedule, keep to it for
    a while, but not long enough for it to become a habit.
    Habits take around 3 weeks to form, so if you want
    your new approach to work and lifestyle to be
    maintained, you must protect it at all costs. If you want
    to achieve your own personal goals, you must protect
    them at all costs. Eventually, the changes you
    implement will become second nature, but until then,
    you need to stay in control of your time management.

"Do not be afraid to experience your emotions; they are the path to your soul. Emotions erupt to remind us we are alive, that we are human. And to let us know we are growing. Trust yourself enough to feel what you feel" - Iyanla Vanzant

Experience Your Emotions But Don't Be Led By Them
Shaisia 'Sparkles' Malachi once asked her audience. "Have you learned to tell the difference between "experiencing your feelings and being led by them"? The answer to this question is very personal and is a question each of us must ask ourselves. True positive thinking and action begin only when we learn to acknowledge and manage our emotions without being overwhelmed by them. People often rely on their instincts or gut feelings when making decisions, and their emotions frequently influence whether they engage in or enjoy certain activities. The challenge with this emotional response is that it's primarily based on feelings rather than logic, even though both can sometimes lead to the same outcome. This is what is meant by *"experiencing your feelings"*. Have you learned to tell the difference between *"experiencing your feelings and being led by them?"*.
By doing so, you can objectively analyze your emotions and then make logical decisions. This skill is especially vital in resolving conflicts, for example, with a spouse or child. In heated moments, it's easy to be swayed by emotions. A wise individual, recognizing the surge of frustration and anger, might suggest a break, allowing for a period of reflection to respond logically instead of emotionally. Identifying the difference between responding emotionally and understanding how our emotions can either help or hinder our actions is crucial for developing a positive mindset.

Negative emotions can trap us, hindering our goals. For example, feelings of unhappiness might drive us to constantly pursue more, depression might result in isolation or overeating, and anger can manifest in harmful attitudes towards loved ones. By learning to redirect these negative emotions towards more constructive decision-making, we can utilize them to guide our behavior choices. However, it's crucial not to let these feelings dictate our actions without first considering alternative, more positive options that can enrich our lives and the decisions we make.

"I can accept failure, but I can't accept not trying."
- Michael Jordan

Setbacks to Success

Many individuals experiment with new ideas, and when things don't work out, they often feel defeated and consider themselves failures. On the other hand, some people push through early difficulties and end up successful. The main difference is in the way they see their experiences. Why do some see value in every result, while others quickly label something a failure if it doesn't bring instant success? The answer is rooted in maintaining an optimistic outlook towards life's experiences. Successes are celebrated as current victories, and failures are seen as building blocks for future achievements. In reality, there are no absolute failures, just steps on the path to ultimate success.

Optimists, who are adept at finding humor in their mistakes and holding onto their grand aspirations, view setbacks not as failures but as opportunities to learn. Taking oneself too seriously can lead to viewing failures as definitive and damaging to self-esteem. However, by celebrating other achievements and seeing a setback as a temporary hurdle, one can maintain optimism. The challenge, then, is to approach failure not as a defeat but as a valuable lesson for the future. How do we embrace this viewpoint and turn our setbacks into opportunities for learning and growth?

1. Challenge what you think of success and failure. It's our perception of them that makes us see failure as negative and success as positive. Failure is simply part of the journey to success, the ultimate destination.

2. When you feel like a failure because of a poor result or outcome, set goals for yourself immediately, deciding how to continue your journey to success. The old, but familiar saying of *"climb back on your horse immediately after you fall off"* is based on this concept.

3. Look at a failure from the perspective of the big picture, not the small picture. You may have not achieved the outcome you wanted, but you did achieve. Make a list of all the things you learned and gained from the experience and celebrate those things. They are achievements, it is not one complete failure, but many small achievements and they deserve to be celebrated. Failure is about opportunity and embracing failure as opportunity helps to eliminate failure from your vocabulary helping you to stay optimistic and find success in everything you do.

CHAPTER EIGHT

ALIGING ENERGIES

BUILDING A LIFE OF BLESSINGS

CHAPTER 8

ALIGNING ENERGIES

BUILDING A LIFE OF BLESSINGS

"Build with belief, and watch your reality bloom into a masterpiece of blessings."

The law of attraction states that our dominant thoughts and feelings attract corresponding experiences. By mastering this immutable law, you become architect of your reality. Consciously direct your mind towards what you wish to manifest - love, prosperity, health. Repeated focus summons these ideals from abstraction into form. Thoughts solidify into things. But first you must sanction only good within your mind's sanctum. Be a vigilant gatekeeper, filtering out negativity before it distorts your energetic magnetism. Dwell only on what you want to attract. You reap what you sow in consciousness. When challenges arise, reframe perspectives to reveal the growth opportunity hidden within. See setbacks as feedback furthering your progress, not failures ending it. Stay future-focused. The present contains shadows only if you face backwards. Similarly, view others through the lens of their highest potential, not their wounds. People reflect back your expectations of them. When you relate to their wholeness, you summon their light. Practice mindfulness to catch negative thought patterns before they calcify. Is your inner monologue affirming or alarmist? Thoughts create filters determining what you perceive. Ensure yours. admittedly liberating possibilities. Meditation cleanses mental clutter to clarify space for inspired visions to arise. Daily quiet the mind's commotion. In stillness, intuition reveals where to focus your energies to magnetize your desired outcomes. Once you know your destination, chart the course with bold faith. Form mental images imbued with senses - taste the victory, smell the success, feel the joy. When you engage your creative imagination, you enlist the full power of mind to build your vision brick by brick. Align your dominant thoughts with positive emotions like love, enthusiasm and optimism. Heart energy magnifies mind power. Passion fuels manifestation. To realize your dreams, dare to desire them wildly, unreasonably. As you broadcast specific intentions through focused thought and feeling, external conditions organize to match your inner blueprint. People and resources align to assist your aims. But you must take the first steps; the universe rewards action, not idle dreaming. While keeping your goals ever in mind, release attachment to how they manifest. The conscious mind maps steps linearly but the universe weaves together miracles mysteriously. Trust in divine timing. Let go of artificial deadlines. Remain open to unexpected blessings. You are learning to work in sync with invisible forces shaping each day. Once you master manifesting small intentions, your confidence in life's magical machinery grows. You need only provide the blueprint. Daily affirm positive expectations about yourself and your world. Thoughts seeking confirmation will discover it. Expect the best and you call it forth. You are the common denominator in every struggle. Turn within when seeking solutions. As your manifestations unfurl, appreciate each milestone. Gratitude amplifies positive energies, accelerating your attracting powers. Relish the journey's gradual miracles, not just the destination. When old thoughts or stories surface to sabotage your resolve, recognize their origin but refuse to own them. They no longer define you. Replace their falsehoods with empowering truths. Your future need not recapitulate your past unless you create it so. You possess the tools within to build a life of blessings by intentionally directing your mind. Master your thoughts and you master your outcomes. Receive what you believe. Create consciously.

"No is a complete sentence." - Shonda Rhimes

Always See The Good In Things
When did you last observe a bee diligently moving from one flower to another, gathering nectar and pollen to nourish the larvae back at the hive? While some bees aren't picky about the plants they visit, others are more selective, focusing on certain species. The honey from these selective bees is prized for its distinctive qualities and flavors.

In the same way, when it comes to life decisions, we can mirror the selective honeybee, embracing beneficial opportunities and steering clear of those that might diminish our wellbeing. Mastering the art of saying no is a valuable, but often overlooked skill. Learning to refuse things that may harm us in the long run is crucial for reducing daily stress and enhancing self-satisfaction and the quality of our decisions. By turning away from harmful elements, we naturally gravitate towards those that are beneficial.

How can you distinguish between what to accept and what to
reject to stay focused and happy? The first step is to pinpoint
the sources of your stress. Enduring stress isn't always
negative; sometimes stepping out of our comfort zone is
necessary for progress. The secret lies in distinguishing
between stress that fosters growth and stress that is
detrimental. This requires a life plan, focusing on accepting
only what aligns with and contributes to this plan.

*"Doesn't matter if the glass is half-empty or half-full.
All that matters is that you are the one pouring the
water" - Mark Cuban*

The Half-Full Glass And Positive People

Have you ever met someone who always seems joyful and
positive , both about themselves and life in general? They
appear to handle life's challenges with calmness and poise.
Do you wish you were more like them and you are able to
deal with your life circumstances like they do?
Such individuals often view life as a "glass half full," finding a
silver lining even when things don't go as planned. While this
outlook comes naturally to some, for many, it's a learned
behavior. It stems from a conscious choice to focus on the
positive rather than dwell on the negative.
Unfortunately, it sounds so easy but in reality, difficult to
execute. How do these people consistently focus on the
positive aspects and maintain their positively? Expressing
gratitude, even in tough situations, is a crucial practice. It's a
cornerstone of optimism and helps in seeing the good in
every situation. Embracing a 'glass half full' mindset involves
carefully evaluating a situation before responding with

negativity. It involves questioning whether complaining will improve or worsen the situation and if it will contribute to solving the problem. Often, the answer is no. Having a clear perspective allows for better resolution of issues. Keeping an attitude of gratitude enables us to view most life events positively, keeping the glass half full, even in the toughest times.

"Life is very interesting. In the end, some of your greatest pains become your greatest strengths."
- Drew Barrymore

Small Things, Big Gifts
We are always surrounded by beauty. The challenge is whether we allow ourselves to see it because life can be very distracting, especially if you live a fast-paced lifestyle. If ever you feel stuck, take a pause to be inspired by your surroundings. Some of the greatest paintings of all times were inspired by everyday scenes. For example, Jean-Michel Basquiat's "Hollywood Africans" in 1983, drew inspiration from the urban landscape and the experiences within it. The thing is that these inspirations are free and ready for you to access whenever you choose. The key is to be present. Here is an effective way to be more present and it is the art of doing things slowly, deliberately and more consciously.

1. Prepare a small assortment of different flavored tea bags in front of you. This activity can be done at any time of the day.

2. When you're ready, choose one tea bag. Take a moment to smell the aroma and feel the texture of the tea bag. Explore it with your senses. The objective is to fully engage with and focus your attention on this single tea bag.

3. Next, slowly brew the tea. As it steeps, observe the color change in the water and inhale the fragrance. When it's ready, take a sip, but don't swallow immediately. Savor the taste of the tea in your mouth, focusing on the flavors rather than the act of drinking.

4. Allocate at least 10 to 15 minutes for this exercise. Although it may seem easy to hurry through something as simple as drinking tea, try to resist the urge. Rushing defeats the purpose of this exercise in mindfulness and presence.

At the conclusion of this exercise, you'll uncover the pleasure found in something as simple as sipping a cup of tea. You'll be amazed by the depth of flavor and aroma that emerges when you concentrate your attention on the present moment. It might seem like a small thing, but don't just take my word for it. Give it a try and experience it yourself. Don't overlook these simple joys.

"Your whole life is a manifestation of the thoughts that go on in your head" - Lisa Nichols

The Law Of Attraction And Your Life

The law of attraction has become a popular concept in our daily lives. It's in high demand because it aligns with our universal wish to see our dreams become reality. Many of us aspire to a life filled with success, accomplishments, and joy, hoping to see our deepest desires fulfilled. The law of attraction offers a way to adjust our thoughts and emotions to attract the kind of life we envision for ourselves.

Here are steps to active the Law of Attraction

Begin by forming a clear and vivid image of the life you wish for. Reflect on your desires, make your requests known to the universe, and create a mental picture. This process involves leveraging your imagination to mold your thoughts, both at the conscious and subconscious levels. Embrace the sensation that your dream is already happening. Then, maintain a positive mindset. Remember, the Law of Attraction weakens in the face of negativity. Nurture a strong belief in your capacity to achieve your goals and consistently reinforce this belief with positive affirmations. Also, practice gratitude and kindness. Cherish what you currently have, share with others, and concentrate on the positives in your life. Such a mindset is key to attracting more positivity and prosperity. Finally, actively pursue your ambitions. Transform your dreams into reality through decisive and courageous actions.

CHAPTER NINE

BRIDGING DREAMS AND REALITY

LEARN TO MANIFEST YOUR DREAMS

CHAPTER 9

BRIDGING DREAMS AND REALITY

LEARN TO MANIFEST YOUR DREAMS

"Listen to your heart's whispers, and keep your inner fire alive."

Within you lies a visionary longing to transform dreams into reality. It's time to unleash this potent creative force within. Boldly design the life you are called to live.

Begin by defining your soul's deepest desires. What vision ignites your passion and purpose? How does your heart wish to contribute using your unique gifts? Make your goals vivid and visceral. Next, take complete ownership of this vision as already yours in energetic form. Speak about your dreams as unfolding certainties rather than distant fantasies. Feel their reality within your bones. When writing your desired outcomes, state them in the present tense as already manifested. Declare to the universe this is what you are - a successful writer, a beloved partner, a world-changer. Claim your identity.

Beware imposter thoughts whispering "Who do you think you are?" to shrink your aspirations. They stem from fears conditioned to play small to stay safe. Thank but disempower them. You contain galaxies. Surround yourself with those who see you, affirm you and reflect back your magnificence - your soul tribe. They will hold your highest self steadily in focus until it becomes your self-image. Let desire be the wind in your sails, not discouragement. Those who achieved excellence did so because they wanted it badly enough. Blaze with single-minded conviction. It magnetizes your visions. The mind may doubt but the heart knows your destiny. Its guidance won't shout but murmurs persistently in moments of stillness. Listen within. Your soul's compass points unwaveringly to your joy. Follow it. When frustration creeps in, renew your sense of excitement and possibility regarding your dreams. They live in the future, beyond current limitations. Nurture your inner fire to glow brightly enough to light your path ahead. Any goal seems impossible if viewed in its entirety. Zoom in on succeeding at just the very next step. Take it. Repeat. Momentum builds, impossible inches to inevitable. Keep advancing. You control only two things - your work ethic and your attitude. Give freely of both and all else aligns in divine timing. Show up consistently with positivity. These daily offerings draw your visions within reach. Bless your efforts and trust your process. Inner riches - wisdom, faith, patience - grow from engaging fully with your purpose. Progress appears non-linear but completes its circuitous journey if allowed. Remember you cannot determine how or when the seeds you plant today will bear fruit. Sow abundantly without attachment to outcomes. Focus on right actions; universe handles miracles.

There will be fallow seasons that feel hopeless but promise rebirth if persevered through consciously. Even the darkest night still cradles stars' guidance if you look inward for their light. This too shall pass. When fear shouts the loudest, lean hardest into love. It dissolves resistance. Love for your craft, love for those you serve, love for the person you are becoming - let it drown out doubt's discordance. Create from this infinite wellspring. You are not defined or bound by the past. Every moment's choice either perpetuates old patterns or liberates you into new possibility. Choose powerfully. Limiting beliefs lose sway once you withdraw belief in them. Progress requires surrender - recognizing you are part of something infinitely grander than your individual will. Align yours with divine will. See life not as happening to but in concert with you. There are no wrong turns, only the long way home. Trust the sureness inside compelling you to grow, contribute, and boldly inhabit your power. It comes from Source. By answering this call, you answer to life's highest purpose: becoming who you were created to be. Say yes. Your destiny awaits.

"If you can dream it, you can do it" -Walt Disney

Achieving Your Dreams

Our thought process plays a big role in our successes. Researchers have said that the concept *"We are what we say we are"* is a statement that we often want to admit. Our state of mind drives our actions. We achieve in life when we can visualize our success. It is at this moment our resolve, determination and confidence kicks in. Don't let yourself spend time focusing on what you can't do, but rather on what you are doing and what you can continue to work on towards your goals and dreams. No one ever achieved anything without dreaming and determining to put the dream into action and succeeding. It cannot be emphasized enough that your thoughts are your worst critic, but it is also your best ally. Your thoughts are partially responsible for your actions and behaviors and most people trust their personal perceptions on things that happen in their lives. Channeling thoughts to bring out the best is essential to reaching personal goals. Surround yourself with people who will support your endeavors and ask them to help you counter your negativity. Nip it in the bud before it has time to blossom into something that causes you to lose your focus. Think of yourself achieving your dreams and you are half way to success.

"I am where I am because I believe in all possibilities." - Whoopi Goldberg

What Are Your Excuses?
All of us have something we really want to do but keep finding excuses not to. Maybe you might want to start a daily walking routine, but household tasks consistently overshadows it. Or you might plan to take up boxing, but work reports keep piling up. We are skilled at justifying why some things seem more important than others. Yet, true life balance involves giving equal importance to our personal aspirations and our responsibilities.

We understand the significance of a diary for scheduling and planning our tasks. Ideally, we'd love to tick off every item on our daily to-do list, but often we find ourselves making excuses for not completing them. When this happens, write down the last five tasks you didn't finish and honestly reflect on the reasons. Your excuses might include feeling too tired, apprehension about doing something alone, or choosing family time over personal hobbies. Remember, these excuses are actually choices we make. Sometimes they're justified, other times they reflect deeper issues in our lives.

By documenting these choices, we're acknowledging our priorities. Why did we skip something? Did we simply opt for another activity? Maybe we adjusted our plans to something more manageable. Understanding our choices helps us change our actions, attitudes, or behaviors to make more beneficial decisions. Ultimately, our choices are crucial in prioritizing our mental, physical, and emotional well-being.

"Peace of mind for five minutes, that's what I crave"
-Alanis Morissette

What You Can Accomplish Within 5 Minutes?

Do you feel like your life is a non-stop rush from one thing to the next? Well, it's time to discover the magic of just five minutes! Even on the busiest days, we can all spare five minutes, and you'd be surprised how much it can transform your day. So, what amazing things can you do in five minutes for self-growth?

Dedicate five minutes daily to tidy up a space. – your desk, pantry, or even the garage. Savor the feeling of accomplishment afterward! A tidy space means a clear mind, and it's proven that clean work areas boost productivity.

Use five minutes for a quick walk. Explore your surroundings and spot something new and beautiful. This little break can help you appreciate the hidden blessings in your busy life.

Squeeze in a five-minute exercise session. Feel the difference in your fitness day by day. Short on time? Six of these mini workouts equal a full 30-minute session!

Spend five minutes in prayer, meditation, or self-reflection to nurture your spiritual health.

Take five minutes to whip up a healthy meal instead of relying on takeout. Your body deserves good nutrition.

Finally, try going to bed five minutes earlier each night. Gradually improving your sleep is key – aim for 7 to 9 hours to stay sharp and focused.

"It does not matter how slowly you go as long as you do not stop" - Confucius

The Lesson Of The Tortoise

Have you heard the classic story of the Tortoise and the Hare? They raced each other, and initially, the hare zoomed ahead, nearly reaching the finish line while the tortoise lagged far behind. But the overconfident hare decided to nap before finishing, and slept so deeply that the tortoise, slowly but surely, crossed the finish line first. The story reminds us that "slow and steady wins the race," and it's true. Both the tortoise and the hare used their natural abilities to the fullest. From a personal growth perspective, this story is quite insightful. The tortoise, though slow, entered the race with determination. He might not have expected to win, but he gave it his all. It wasn't just a leisurely stroll for him; he pushed his limits and, surprisingly, it led to his victory. The hare, with all his speed, should have easily won, but his overconfidence was his downfall. He became arrogant, and that cost him the race. This fable teaches us important life lessons. The tortoise, doing his best within his limits, didn't let the challenge daunt him and found success. The hare, despite his talent, self-satisfaction to get the better of him, leading to his failure. It's worth pondering – in our own lives, do we succeed by adopting the tortoise's attitude, or do we falter like the hare, resting on our past achievements instead of pushing through to the end?

"We all have dreams. In order to make dreams come into reality, it takes an awful lot of determination, dedication, self-discipline, and effort." - Jesse Owens

Positive Thinking And Determination

Positive thinking is key, yet it's just the first step in the uninterrupted journey of discovering who you truly are. You need to take action based on your thoughts and beliefs, and this is where willpower plays a major role. Making decisions and persistently chasing your goals requires willpower, a powerful force. When combined with determination and a clear purpose, you become an unstoppable force. However, faltering at the first hurdle means you might never reach your goals due to a lack of willpower. Consider Nelson Mandela, who spent 27 years in prison fighting for South Africa's freedom. His unwavering conviction and willpower were essential in sustaining him through such a challenging time. Everyone possesses willpower, but it needs to be strengthened and harnessed. Here are three steps to boost and utilize your willpower:

- Recognize Your Boundaries. Identify an area for improvement, such as health and fitness, which is accessible and shows tangible results with consistency. Choose a specific activity, like running, weightlifting, or rope skipping. Track your performance each time you engage in this activity.

- Challenge Yourself. After you've measured your results a few times, the next step is to push beyond your limits. If you've been running 5 miles in 90 minutes consistently, try to finish in a shorter time. Set a goal, prepare for it, and go for it.

- Celebrate Your Efforts! After each attempt to push your limits, celebrate your achievement, regardless of whether you met your goal. Celebrating creates positive associations with exercising your willpower and expanding your boundaries. And when you finally hit your target? Celebrate even more!

By following these steps, you'll condition yourself to break through your limitations, making it an enjoyable and rewarding process.

CHAPTER TEN

CHANGES OF LIFE

MOVING FORWARD:BREAKING FREE FROM PAST LIMITATIONS

CHAPTER 10

CHANGES OF LIFE

"Embrace change as the sculptor of your destiny, for within its challenges lies the chisel that carves the masterpiece of your life"

Consider this: the secret to change is not solely about eliminating undesirable behaviors. Instead, it lies in focusing on the behaviors we wish to cultivate. Those who seem to effortlessly embrace change possess a burning desire deep within their subconscious. This desire fuels their journey and minimizes the pain of transformation. To embark on this transformative path, we must first examine the factors influencing our behavior, bridging the gap between our conscious and subconscious minds. Have you ever found yourself struggling to change despite your best efforts? Seeking help from counselors, psychologists, or investing in self-help seminars may have left you feeling stuck in the same place. This is because our habits exert a powerful influence over our lives. To break free, we must become acutely aware of these habits and replace the negative ones with constructive alternatives.

Begin by crafting a list that outlines your perceptions and attitudes toward life. Recognize that not all of these serve you well, and that's perfectly okay. The key is to eliminate the detrimental perceptions and replace them with their positive counterparts. Your subconscious mind absorbs these perceptions, turning them into self-fulfilling prophecies. So, instead of dwelling on discouragement or unfavorable circumstances, focus on your past achievements or visualize the potential that lies ahead. It may feel unfamiliar at first, but persistence is key. Even if it takes time, keep practicing until it leads you towards your dreams.

Remember, this process requires unwavering dedication. Giving up is not an option. Keep nurturing those positive attributes until they guide you unswervingly toward your goals. Habits can be both our allies and adversaries. While it's common to think of habits as negative forces, they can also be sources of immense benefit. The key to forming and sustaining healthy habits lies in consistency and discipline. In a mere three weeks, a new habit can become second nature, effortlessly integrated into your daily routine.

To make this transition, shift your new habits from conscious actions to subconscious routines. For instance, if you aspire to walk for half an hour before work each morning, set a fixed time and stick to it religiously. After three weeks, skipping that morning walk will feel like an omission from your daily ritual. Understand that there may be moments of weakness in your journey, where your resolve wavers. When this happens, focus on leaving those moments behind and restarting without hesitation. Patience and consistency will ultimately lead to the successful establishment of your new, healthy life habits. How do you perceive yourself today? Do you believe that losing weight or acquiring material possessions will bring happiness and fulfillment? Often, we tie our self-worth to external factors, living in a perpetual state of longing for a better future. To break free from this mindset, we must challenge these thoughts. Our self-worth should not be contingent on future achievements or acquisitions. Instead, we must learn to appreciate and love ourselves as we are in the present. By embracing the opportunities and resources within us now, we pave the way for future achievements. It is only when we truly love and accept ourselves in the present that every accomplishment becomes a cause for celebration. Life is a series of changes, some of which can be monumental and life-altering. When betrayal or disappointment strikes, it's easy to lose trust in others and question our decision-making abilities. However, dwelling on the past and letting it dictate our future is a path to stagnation.

"Excellence is not a singular act, but a habit. You are what you do repeatedly." - Shaquille O'Neal

Why Is Changing a Habit So Difficult?

Breaking habits means stepping out of your comfort zone, which is often a challenging task, no matter how eager we are for change. Many of us want to alter certain habits, whether they're physical, mental, spiritual, or emotional. These habits are deeply embedded in our minds, making change seem like a formidable task. To successfully change, focus on the behavior you wish to adopt, rather than the one you want to leave behind.

Have you ever wondered why change comes easily to some but not to others? The key lies in your subconscious desire. When you deeply desire a change at a subconscious level, achieving it becomes less painful. The first step is to reflect on the issues influencing your behavior and perception. This reflection helps align your conscious and subconscious minds, leading to significant accomplishments. Jot down those limiting beliefs that are stopping you from growing. Keep revisiting and tweaking them. This process is all about challenging what's holding you back. Once you pinpoint the exact behavior you're ready to transform, let's dive into strategies to kickstart and maintain this exciting change.

Pre-contemplation: In this initial phase, people haven't realized there's a problem and often steer clear of the topic. Contemplation: Now, they're aware of the issue but hesitant about changing. They know things could be better, but they haven't taken the leap yet.

Preparation: Here, people are on the brink of change. They're not all in yet, but they're getting ready, often driven by the pressure of their current situation.

Action: This is when the real change kicks in. It's time to put plans into motion.

Maintenance: The challenge now is to keep up with these new changes. Staying on track is key to avoid starting over from square one.

"Motivation is what gets you started. Habit is what keeps you going." - Jim Ryun

Changing Habits That Are Deeply-Rooted

Have you ever felt stuck, unable to change a habit even after lots of thinking and trying? Maybe you've even sought professional help or attended self-help seminars, only to find yourself back where you started. This happens because our habits deeply root themselves in our lives. That's why recognizing and replacing negative habits with positive ones is so important. If you're not hitting your goals, it's time to reevaluate how you approach life. Start by making a list of your views and attitudes. Sure, you'll find some that aren't helping you, but don't be too hard on yourself. The trick is to completely let go of these unhelpful thoughts and replace them with positive ones. Your subconscious absorbs your beliefs, turning them into self-fulfilling prophecies. So, instead of discouraging thoughts, focus on your past successes and how much more you can achieve. Even if it doesn't feel true right away, keep at it. It's about 'faking it till you make it', no matter how long it takes. This practice demands your wholehearted commitment, or you might be tempted to quit early. Keep feeding your mind positive thoughts until they naturally guide you towards your dreams.

"The only person you are destined to become is the person you decide to be."
- Ralph Waldo Emerson

A Healthy Living Habit

We often view habits as negative, things we do without thinking even though we'd rather not. However, it's important to remember that habits can be both positive and negative, with good habits being beneficial for us. Habits typically take three weeks to form. Whether it's changing your lifestyle, eating differently, or committing to a daily walk, these can become second nature with consistent effort. Discipline makes maintaining these new habits easier. The secret to establishing these positive habits is to transition them from conscious actions to subconscious routines, something you do automatically. Take, for example, the goal of walking for half an hour before work each day. Stick to your scheduled time religiously. After three weeks, skipping a walk will feel like something's missing from your morning routine. It's natural to experience moments of weakness when trying to form new habits. When these moments occur, it's crucial to move past them and restart without delay. With perseverance and consistency, you'll find success in creating new, healthy life habits.

"Don't be pushed around by the fears in your mind. Be led by the dreams in your heart" - Roy T. Bennett

Take a moment and reflect on how you feel about yourself right now. Are you caught up in thoughts that losing weight will bring you ultimate happiness? Or perhaps you're dreaming of that flashy new car, imagining the admiration of your friends? It's common to tie our self-image to our appearance and possessions. But let's be honest, that mindset is more about living for a future 'better' self than appreciating who we are now. This "life will be better when..." attitude needs a serious rethink. If we don't start loving ourselves as we are, we'll always be chasing an elusive future for self-improvement. The truth is, everything we need to be our best selves already lies within us. If your goal is to lose weight, make sure it's for you and not for anyone else. Otherwise, the journey might lead nowhere. Dwelling on the future can stall our personal growth and achievements. Instead, seize today's opportunities – they're your stepping stones to future successes. Remember, your worth isn't measured by your actions. The key to true fulfillment lies in embracing and valuing yourself as you are now. Otherwise, you risk downplaying your own successes. If we set unrealistic expectations and don't meet them, our self-esteem suffers, and we lose the drive to explore and grow. However, by grounding our self-worth in self-acceptance, every single achievement, big or small, becomes a victory worth celebrating.

"Change is the law of life. And those who look only to the past or present are certain to miss the future
- John F. Kennedy

Reflect on this: have you ever experienced a significant event in your life? When we're hurt or let down by those close to us, it's common to start thinking we can't trust anyone again. A few negative experiences can send us spiraling into a negative path, shaking our confidence in making good choices. Dwelling in the past, allowing it to control our future, is often why many feel stuck and unable to move forward. This is where acknowledging the past becomes crucial — it's the first step in healing and moving towards a brighter future. Always keep in mind your self-worth, regardless of the changes coming your way. If past events are impacting your current life, consider seeking help from a professional or a religious leader, especially if you have faith in the Most High.

Ready to empower yourself? Here's how:

❖ Remember, the past is just that – past. No words or actions can alter what's already happened. Once you realize the past might be the source of your negative thoughts, it's time to shift them into something positive. Think of it as a fresh start.

❖ Challenge yourself to envision a new you, not who you were, but who you aspire to be. Grab a pen and sketch out your life a decade from now, but write it as if it's happening right now. Make it a regular habit to read this vision and watch how it evolves. You might just find yourself amazed by the transformation.

"To be prepared is half the victory" - Miguel de Cervantes

Anticipating & Preparing For Change

Change is a constant in our lives. Sometimes it's an exciting journey we eagerly anticipate, complete with enjoyable preparations. Yet at other times, change hits us unexpectedly, leaving us distressed and unprepared, often causing both mental disarray and physical reactions that feel beyond our control. Adopting a mindset ready for unplanned change can help us navigate through these trouble times, even when things seem wildly out of our hands. Embracing the inevitability of change encourages us to ponder and prepare for it long before it occurs. This preparation isn't just about facing the inevitable; it's about learning to manage our reactions to stress and disruption effectively.

Planning for change isn't tempting fate; it's accepting reality. Consider professionals who deal with sudden emergencies. They're always in a state of readiness, trained to anticipate various scenarios and respond effectively, aiming to prevent or reduce harm. We can take a leaf out of their book, applying similar strategies to our lives to prepare for change and potential stress.

There are three key ways to brace ourselves for change:

First off, remember this: the higher the chance of something happening, the more you should be gearing up for it. Take people living in natural disaster zones, for example. Every year, they get their homes and minds ready, fully expecting that something might happen.

Now, let's bust a myth: you absolutely can prep your mind for big life changes. Sure, you can't predict everything, like what being a new parent feels like. But you can still arm yourself with knowledge and identify areas where you might face challenges in your new role.

And here's the kicker: dealing with small day-to-day changes? That's like training for the big leagues. Every time you successfully navigate a little bump in the road, you're building the skills to tackle those huge, out-of-the-blue changes. It's like life's own boot camp for the unexpected!

Here's To A Powerful Manifestation
In wrapping up this journey of self-discovering who you truly are uninterrupted, and unlocking the depths of your subconscious, congratulations are in order! Remember, There

is potential in you. Every virtue and power within you is ready to come to life, fueling your existence. No matter your current situation or how you perceive yourself, you possess every right to achieve your goals. Each person is deserving of all the success the world can offer. As you begin to apply the insights from this journey, watch as your fears and insecurities fade away, replaced by courage and wisdom. These will be your trusted companions on this incredible adventure. Your journey begins with envisioning your dream. Cling to your faith and belief; they are the tools that will sculpt your path to triumph. Cheers to your powerful and successful journey ahead.

❖ **The Endless Journey**

As we reach the conclusion of "Who Are You, Uninterrupted?," it's a moment to pause and acknowledge the profound journey you've embarked upon. This adventure into the depths of your subconscious mind has been more than just a quest for knowledge; it's been a voyage towards self-realization. You've embarked into uncharted territories of your inner self, unraveling layers of thoughts, beliefs, and emotions, each step bringing you closer to the core of who you truly are. Uninterrupted self-discovery is a courageous journey, one that requires honesty, vulnerability, and self-reflection. By engaging in this process, you've taken significant strides in understanding and embracing the complexities of your identity. This book has aimed to be a guiding light, illuminating paths in the intricate network of the subconscious, helping you decode the language of your inner world. As you close this chapter, remember that the journey of self-discovery is ongoing. The depths of your subconscious are a universe in themselves, constantly evolving and revealing new truths. Embrace this journey with an open heart and mind, and let your uninterrupted self continue to unfold and manifest in all its glory.

Here's to you, in your most authentic and uninterrupted form, embarking on a continuous journey of self-awareness and fulfillment. May the insights you've gained be the compass that guides you towards a life of deeper meaning and purpose. Keep exploring, keep questioning, and keep growing – for the journey to self-discovery is a journey without end. To your unending journey of discovering in *Who Are You, Uninterrupted* – may you always find joy in the endless quest to know and love yourself, just as you are.

About The Author

Stephanie 'Liberty' Francois is a visionary author whose work is transforming the landscape of self-discovery and personal growth. With a profound commitment to inspiring individuals to unlock their fullest potential, she has crafted "Who Are You, Uninterrupted?" as a pivotal chapter in an ongoing narrative of growth and enlightenment. Through her writing, Liberty guides readers on a transformative journey to shed limiting beliefs, embrace a life of optimism, and live with a purpose that is both intentional and authentic. Liberty's unique approach combined with deep self-reflection with actionable insights, creating a powerful tool for anyone looking to master the intricate dance of the human experience. As an author, she is more than just a storyteller; she is a beacon of hope and a catalyst for change, encouraging each reader to embark on their own journey of self-discovery and to embrace the endless possibilities that lie within. With each word, Liberty is not only writing a book but also building a legacy—one that empowers others to live their most fulfilled lives.

115

©The Finest

"A JOURNEY WHERE YOU'RE THE EXPLORER OF YOUR OWN SOUL.
LIGHTING UP THE WORLD WITH YOUR UNIQUE SPARK."

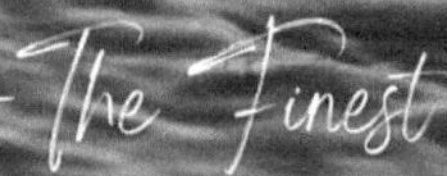

www.ingramcontent.com/pod-product-compliance
Lightning Source LLC
Chambersburg PA
CBHW040908110726
48005CB00006B/836